The Princeton Review

Job Notes:

Networking

The Princeton Review

Job Notes: Networking

BY MARGARET HEENEHAN, M.ED.

Random House, Inc.
New York 1997
http://www.randomhouse.com

Princeton Review Publishing, L.L.C.
2315 Broadway, 2nd Floor
New York, NY 10024
e-mail: info@review.com

 Published in the United States by Random House, Inc., New York, and simultaneously in Canada by Random House of Canada Limited, Toronto.

ISBN 0-679-77175-1

Editor: Amy E. Zavatto
Designer: Illeny Maaza

Manufactured in the United States of America on partially recycled paper.

9 8 7 6 5 4 3 2 1

First Edition

Dedication

To my family, friends, and clients who make my life so incredibly rich and continue to teach me the important lessons of life.

Contents

Introduction

So, you're conducting your first job search or initiating another one.

You have a beautiful new interview outfit and a killer resume. You've worked hard to investigate possible contact organizations through the library and your high school or college career center, and you have spent hours sifting through the newspaper for job advertisements in your field of interest. Over the last two months you've sent out over thirty resumes without so much as a nibble from prospective employers. Worse yet, you're running out of ideas and enthusiasm. What's wrong????

Many people become so intent on the job search that they end up conducting it in a vacuum. This isn't to say that they aren't on top of things; they're simply unaware of a very important component of the process. For instance, Leticia, a college senior, was in a position similar to the one described above. She had worked very hard throughout her senior year researching the type of industry she wanted to pursue, and had dutifully read every resume and cover letter book she could get her hands on. But as she neared her graduation date, she was still without a job and had only a few interviews. She was near tears because she was so frustrated with the lack of response in her job search, and was even questioning her career choice.

When I saw Leticia in a counseling appointment I asked her to walk me through her job search process. We reviewed her resume and I proofread several cover letters that she had sent out. No problems there. She also obviously "knew her stuff" about the field of arts administration, the area she wanted to pursue, and filled me in on the hours she had spent poring over books and articles on the topic. But, when I asked her if she had actually spoken to anyone in the field, I was met with a blank stare. "What do you mean?" she asked. "I've spoken to librarians at the public library where I did my research, if that's what you're talking about," she added. Bingo! We had identified the "hole" in her job search.

Leticia had worked very hard to prepare for her first job, but she had unintentionally omitted an extremely important part of the job search. While books and periodicals can do wonders in describing a particular position, talking with people can do this and far more. Making contact with people in a particular field can give you an insider's view of a job and/or organization, provide additional leads or contacts for your job search, and help you build confidence in the interviewing process.

The term "networking" is used to describe the process of making contact with people in your field of interest and is a vital part of the job search process. This book was written not only to describe networking, but to identify how to use it most effectively when conducting a job search. It highlights the ways in which to identify career contacts (even if you feel you don't have any) as well as the method by which you can figure out your own "networking style." But unlike many other books on the topic which simply identify the term, it explains how to use and maintain your career network, from first contact through follow-up. Each chapter also includes some of the most frequently asked questions about the whole process.

And lastly, throughout the book I will discuss how technology and the Internet are changing the face of networking, offering yet another dimension to the networking process.

1

Networking—Uncovering Job Search Opportunities

How Networking Can Work For You

Some of you may be familiar with the term "networking," while others may not be sure exactly what it means. The term is used so much to describe a variety of activities that its meaning has become muddled. For instance, how do you actually "network"? Does the term mean seeking out people and asking them for jobs? Should you network with everybody you meet? Do you network with people you already know? Networking is such a buzz word in the world of job search, yet for many it remains an ambiguous term.

Simply stated, a network can be defined as a system of interconnected pathways or relationships. We all have many different relationships in our lives.These relationships can be personal or professional and, in some cases, may overlap. Your personal network probably includes parents, siblings, relatives, and friends. These are the people whose lives connect with yours on some basic level and who support you in your daily endeavors.

Now let's take the term and relate it to your job search or, in other words, your professional life. Here it means connecting with a variety of people who can, in some direct or indirect way, assist you in finding a job or determining a career. Now, in some cases, your personal contacts can offer tips for your professional life. Or, you may seek out people who you do not know well enough (if at all) to provide the same kind of advice. And, in fact, searching out virtual strangers for career advice is perfectly acceptable and is a normal part of the networking process.

Whether it means giving you information about a particular industry, offering job leads, or providing you with more people to speak with, networking contacts can offer vital assistance. Plain and simple, *networking is one of the most important components of career research and the job search*. Think about it. It doesn't take a rocket scientist to figure out that the more people you know, the more information you gather, and the more you're "out there," the better your chances are of finding employment, provided you do it in the right way.

I'm kind of shy and have a hard time meeting people. What do I do?

It's important to find the networking style that's right for you. For example, if calling someone first with no previous introduction makes you a nervous wreck, consider writing a letter first and following up with a phone call. Also consider the best networking arena for you. Some are more comfortable in one-to-one structured meetings, while others feel more at ease at a football game.

By starting out with just two people, you could possibly increase your job search network by four if you simply ask each of those individuals for two additional networking contacts. This way you're expanding the number of people who can offer you professional advice. It's pretty amazing how quickly you can create and strengthen a network to assist you with your job search, provided you ask the right questions.

What You Can Expect to Gain

All right, so networking is supposed to help with the career research and the job search. But how, exactly? What information can you expect to walk away with from a networking experience? Why can't you just read up on a particular career field and be done with it?

My aunt said she can get me a job at the local health center. Do I still have to network? FAQ

Networking is always a valuable tool. Who knows, the job with your aunt might not pan out. At the very least, you can talk to others in that sector who can give you their take on working for a health organization and, while you're at it, make some other contacts in the field. You can even bone up on your interviewing skills and trends in the field. The bottom line is: "Cover your bases."

Networking can serve a variety of purposes; that's the beauty of the whole process. For instance, networking can:

1. **Help you narrow down your career choices**
   Pilar was not sure if she wanted to pursue a career in public relations or marketing. The fields seemed so similar and yet different. She read a lot about the fields and they both sounded interesting. The counselor at her school career center suggested she speak with people in the field, so she met with some alums in the industry. After speaking with them she realized that the jobs were very different and decided that public relations was more in tune with her interests.

2. **Assist in validating your career choice**
Samuel had always thought he wanted to follow in his grandfather's footsteps and pursue a career in medicine. He liked his science courses and excelled in them. But before taking that big leap, he wanted to talk to some people who were working in the field. While in school he met with some friends of his parents who were doctors, and asked them questions about their work. He even spent some time volunteering at the local hospital's emergency room. He absolutely loved the frenetic pace of the ER and felt gratified by the work. These experiences only reinforced his decision to pursue a career in medicine.

3. **Get you advice about your job search**
Someone who is in your field of interest can give you some ideas about what works and what doesn't in your quest for a job. I once knew a client who was interested in becoming a paralegal. He went to his university's law school and spent hours reading books that identified the top law firms in his preferred geographic location. He also met with his mother's friend, a lawyer with one of those firms. When he told her that he was thinking about doing a mass mailing of his resume to all of the law firms in the area, she suggested a more targeted mailing, focusing only on the firms specializing in environmental law, his area of interest. She even gave him some helpful hints for improving his resume.

4. **Give you information about a particular company**
You can read a great deal of literature about certain companies. But remember, it's usually the companies themselves who provide the information for many of the publications you read. Consequently, some of the information may be slanted to present the company in the best possible light. Also, company literature can be "old" before it even goes to press. While I'm not suggesting that you ignore much of the literature found at

your local libraries or college career centers, I am recommending that you also talk to people about a particular industry or organization. Networking contacts or industry insiders can provide vital information that can't be found in some of these publications.

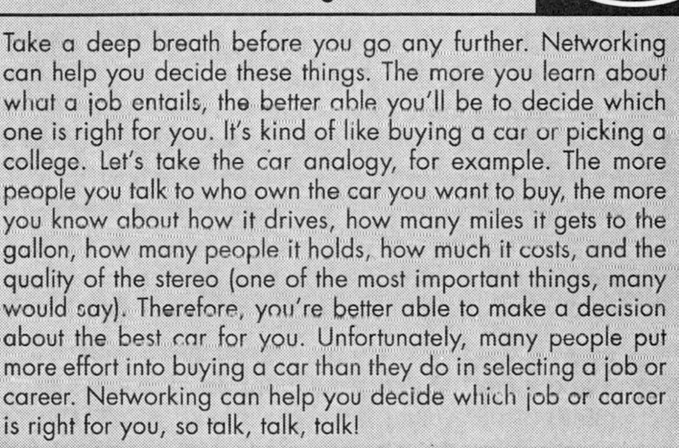

What happens if I'm TOTALLY confused about the career I want to get into?

FAQ

Take a deep breath before you go any further. Networking can help you decide these things. The more you learn about what a job entails, the better able you'll be to decide which one is right for you. It's kind of like buying a car or picking a college. Let's take the car analogy, for example. The more people you talk to who own the car you want to buy, the more you know about how it drives, how many miles it gets to the gallon, how many people it holds, how much it costs, and the quality of the stereo (one of the most important things, many would say). Therefore, you're better able to make a decision about the best car for you. Unfortunately, many people put more effort into buying a car than they do in selecting a job or career. Networking can help you decide which job or career is right for you, so talk, talk, talk!

I should warn here that it can be dangerous to base your thoughts and decisions on only one person's opinion about a particular career field. Remember that individual opinions can be slanted, too. That's why it's best to speak with several industry people to get more well-rounded information.

5. **Give information about how your skills are relevant to a certain industry**

   Networking contacts can provide useful information about how your experiences relate to a particular industry and how to best present yourself on a resume and in an interview. For instance, Sasha once told me how a networking contact told her to highlight a public speaking course she had in college when applying for jobs in real estate. Sasha had thought the course irrelevant and had not even thought to include it on her resume!

6. **Tell you what a particular job might involve**
   Books and journals can tell you about the duties involved in a wide range of careers, but there's nothing better than someone with the actual job title or in a related field filling you in on the details! A young college man I knew was very interested in pursuing a career in investment banking upon graduation. He knew it was an extremely competitive field with an excellent salary. He decided to attend an alumni networking meeting, which focused on careers in finance, at his college career center. After hearing several alums detailing their typical eighty to ninety-hour work weeks, however, he found himself reconsidering his options. While he was still interested in the field, he wanted a job that would offer more balance with his personal life.

7. **Allow you to research trends in your field of interest**
   You can use the networking opportunity to determine both short and long-term industry trends. This information can be helpful when deciding on a career, and also when actually interviewing for jobs, where you can show your knowledge of the field.

8. **Possibly uncover hidden job openings or create new ones**
   Although it's unwise to approach a networking opportunity with the assumption that your contact will find you a job, it has happened. I once worked with a young client in her mid-twenties who so impressed her networking contact that he mentioned her to the CEO of his company. Because she had extensive computer experience and the CEO was interested in expanding in the area of information systems, he asked to speak with her and eventually hired her.

Ultimately, it's hoped that such experiences will lead to consideration for job openings, but you shouldn't walk into a networking meeting expecting this to happen.

9. **Help you polish your interviewing skills**
   The bottom line here is "practice makes perfect." People right out of high school or college generally haven't spent much time in interviewing situations. Short of the "interviews" I had to work at a local deli during summer months or my meetings with admissions counselors during college visits, I was very green about the whole process when I graduated. Consequently, networking opportunities can provide much needed experience in how to talk about yourself and your career goals.

10. **Increase your number of contacts**
    As I mentioned earlier, the more people you know, the better your chances of uncovering job opportunities. So, if you make a point of asking each networking contact for one or two other people to speak with, you're increasing your contact base and your own visibility in the field. This exposure, provided it's done in the correct way, can only increase your chances of finding a job.

I know that networking can increase my number of contacts. How do I actually do it?

When speaking with a networking contact, it's fine to end the discussion by asking, "Would you know of one or two other people who I could speak to who are in this or a related field?" Explain that you're interested in gathering more information for your job/career search. You'd be surprised at how willing people are to help out and would be happy to offer some additional contacts.

As you can see, networking serves a number of purposes when conducting career research for your job search. It's not merely "schmoozing" or "sucking up to people," as many of you may think.The important thing is to take advantage of the numerous opportunities it can provide.

Who Are Your Networking Contacts?

When discussing networking, the most common response I hear is "But I don't know anybody." As a student, recent graduate, or someone looking for a new job, you might feel your list of personal contacts is too short; or, you might not even know one person in the field in which you want to work, so you figure you're done for. Let me start by saying that everyone knows somebody! Granted, your aunt may not head the Fortune 500 company you would like to work for but, if you're creative, you can come up with at least a handful of initial networking contacts.

How can I make contacts if I don't know one person in my field of interest? FAQ

Be creative about how you search for contacts. As I said, this often means thinking outside the box. If at first you can't find anyone in graphic arts, for example, think of another way to go about your search. You might have a cousin who is employed by an organization in the same building as a graphic arts firm that you'd be interested in working for. See if your cousin is familiar with anyone who works with the company. For instance, perhaps your cousin rides the elevator with an administrative assistant at the graphic arts firm (hey, you never know). Remember, you're putting together a string of connections. The person you eventually talk to may not even know your cousin, but the funny thing about networking is that it doesn't matter. As long as you have a name to give to people, even if it's through a series of contacts, that's what matters. Also, try your school alums and/or some professional associations with a focus on graphic artists.

Even if you're starting with very few connections, you can network successfully. Most individuals focus their search for networking contacts on those people immediately surrounding them. "Well, my mother or uncle or cousin doesn't know anyone in my field, so I'm sunk." The trick is to delve beyond the first layer of contacts and use your imagination. Let's say you've decided to pursue a career in the music industry. In trying to find contacts, you've asked your mom (are you kidding?), your sister (she's in the seventh grade), and even your grandfather (who knows nothing more recent than Benny Goodman) if they know anybody who works in the music business and they don't. What do you do next? You delve beyond the first layer.

Is the goal of networking to meet as many people as I can?

Both quality AND quantity matter. You won't win the lottery or get a job simply by being the first among your friends to accumulate 1,000 contact names. While the number of connections you make is certainly important, never let the quantity of contacts take precedence over the quality of contacts. Be sure that every contact is made with courtesy and tact, and make sure that your strategy is appropriate.

For instance, you may know someone who works at the school radio station. Although this person probably won't be your contact with the president of Sony Records, she may know someone at a small independent label who has been in contact with her, trying to promote some local bands. Or, in checking out your college alumni directory, you may discover an alum who is an entertainment lawyer. Although she doesn't work at a record label, she may very well have contacts in the field. If you think creatively, networking contacts can be found in a bunch of places. Just learn to think outside the usual box.

Ask and I Shall Tell You

If you're new at this or returning to the process of looking for a new job, it can be hard to come up with a list of contacts. If there's one helpful hint I can provide, it's this: Ask! Ask teachers and professors (both present and past), ask friends, even ask the owners of your local video store (believe me, they know a bunch of people!). Ask anyone you come in contact with in your daily routine. You'd be surprised at how the most tenuous of acquaintances are willing to give you names of people to talk to.

In an effort to make your job a little easier, the following list provides possible resources for the networking game. By no means a finite list, it's a place to begin and work from. These contacts can include:

1. **Family/extended family**
   Use your parents, guardians, siblings, grandparents, aunts, uncles, and/or cousins as possible resources. Again, try to remember to look beyond the obvious. A woman I worked with, who wanted a job in advertising, once told me that her parents, who owned a shoe store, didn't know anyone at all in the field and couldn't provide her with any networking contacts. She felt that because her mom and dad had immigrated to this country only ten years before, they would be of little help. After a little more discussion though, she realized that her parents were in touch with a variety of sneaker company representatives, and those reps could put her in touch with some contacts in their respective advertising departments. Pretty interesting, huh?

2. **Friends/acquaintances**
   This category includes friends, friends of friends, parents of friends, and people in your apartment building or neighborhood. It may feel awkward to approach these people, but remember, you're not asking for a job. Rather, you're just looking for people to talk to who are in a particular field.

3. **Coworkers and employers, past and present**
   If your job search is being done on the sly and you don't want your boss to know about it, be very careful. There's often nothing worse than your employer knowing you want out before you actually are. But past and present colleagues could be

good sources of networking information, even if they are in a seemingly unrelated field.

4. **Teachers and professors, past and present**
Remember Mr. Cottrell from your senior English class? Or Professor Ramirez from your accounting course? These people can be great resources in the job search, even if you graduated several years ago. Educators can be excellent sources for contacts, particularly if you have had a good rapport with them.

5. **Alumni/ae of your high school(s) and college(s)**
These contacts can be extremely helpful. Of course, getting in touch with these people will be contingent on the quality of your high school's or college's career centers and/or alumnae affairs offices. In addition to individual listings for alums, many schools organize alumni/ae receptions throughout the year, so it's always wise to inquire about such opportunities when contacting your school(s). Most schools will have their graduates categorized by career area and geographic location, so if you're considering moving to another city or state, it may be helpful to find out if there are alums in that area. Besides physically visiting them, you can also network with distant alums through email.

6. **High school or college counselors and advisers**
This category could include career counselors, deans, and college activities officers. Many high schools and most colleges have career development offices that can be invaluable sources for networking information. Counselors in these offices can provide useful tips and point you to valuable resources and contacts. It's wise to "make nice" with these administrators if you're still in school. Some college and university career centers even have home pages on the World Wide Web that offer this information. So, if you've graduated and live far from your alma mater, you can still gain access to valuable information.

7. **Clubs or organizations to which you belong**
   If still in school, do you participate in student government or the economics club? Talking to other members of these organizations can often yield important networking results. Or, if you're out of school, do you belong to the local women's cooperative or SPCA? People who are involved in a common interest can often have great information to share with each other.

8. **Health clubs or sports teams**
   People in these organizations may have contacts in your field of interest. Just think, you may ultimately have found a use for the obnoxious guy on your intramural softball team.

9. **Religious organizations**
   Churches, temples, or other religious organizations can be a rich resource, offering a wide array of contacts in a variety of career fields. I once knew a man who found fifteen contacts in architecture (a profession he was pursuing) through his synagogue's membership list!

10. **Your doctor, dentist, banker, and anyone else who works with you and other people**
    Although it may seem bizarre to ask for referrals while getting your teeth cleaned, it's perfectly appropriate. And think about the number of possible contacts (or sets of teeth) your dentist might know! You may also want to contact the local chamber of commerce for a list of employers in your geographic area of interest.

11. **People you don't know but who do work that interests you**
    Maybe you read an article about a successful civil engineer in your area, and you're interested in entering that field. Try writing that person a letter. It may feel weird to do this, but you'd be surprised how others may respond. Many people enjoy the

attention and recognition, or may simply be interested in helping out.

12. **Professional associations**
These organizations can include, but are certainly not limited to, the American Medical Association, the American Association of University Women, the NAACP, or the Asian American Journalists Association. Very often these associations have a list of members divided up by geographic location. A selected list of associations has been included in chapter 2. In addition, these associations can be found in the yellow pages of the phone book, in professional trade journals, or in *The Encyclopedia of Associations*, which can be found at your college career center or your local library. Try writing to the organization or, if possible, attending one of their meetings.

13. **Telephone books and directories**
Whether you're looking for work close to home or conducting a long-distance job search, the local phone book for your desired destination is an excellent source of information related to your career field. Phone books for most major American cities can be found at branches of the public library or at your career development center (depending on the quality of the office, of course). Once you've targeted certain organizations, you may want to call and find out the names of key people at those organizations.

14. **Newspapers**
In addition to phone books, you may want to subscribe to the local paper to help you get acquainted with key players and organizations, as well get a peek at the ebb and flow of the "help wanted" section for that area.

Newspapers also list career fairs, among other networking opportunities. The terms "career fair," "employment fair," and "job fair" are interchangeable terms used to describe an event where a large number of employers congregate to interview possible job candidates.The career fair may not be your idea of a good time, but it can be most helpful when networking for the job search. Where else can you find upwards of 100 organizations in the same physical space looking for people to hire?

15. **Career/Job Fairs**
    Career/job fairs are typically held by college career centers or a consortium of organizations with a particular focus or interest. There are not-for-profit fairs, business/financial service fairs, and minority career fairs, to name a few. The purpose of these fairs is to get the largest number of job candidates into the same room with the largest number of organizations with positions to fill. Pretty wild, huh? Consequently, you can network with a large number of people with very little running around.

16. **The Internet**
    The Internet has a wide range of networking opportunities, including mailing lists, bulletin boards, newsgroups, chat groups, and individual E-mail accounts. Even if you don't have your own computer, you can usually gain access to one through your local library or school career center.

Hopefully, this list will provide you with a starting point for your networking search. When creating your personalized network, try to use a variety of these resources rather than simply focusing on one. In fact, you may think of some unique contacts of your own, and I encourage you to pursue them.

The Informational Interview

Now that you're aware of the different ways to generate networking contacts, you need to know what to do with them. Do you have to invite these people to dinner or a soccer game, investing thousands of dollars cultivating networking contacts? Have no fear, networking doesn't have to be an expensive venture!

The most effective way to network, with respect to time and money, is to conduct "informational interviews." Informational interviews are meant to help you do just that—gather information for career research and the job search. Through interviews or meetings with people, you can find out what a particular job involves, how to find those jobs, and ways to prepare yourself for the job search. Informational interviews are usually limited to one meeting, and require preparation on the part of (you) the interviewer. They are not job interviews and should not be used to ask for a job (although you may hope it will ultimately lead to one). Rather, it's a way in which to discover pathways to particular jobs or careers. Research the person, the organization, and the career field wherever possible.

Informational interviews are typically thirty minutes to one hour in duration, and you should request that amount of time when contacting people. The interviews themselves can be conducted in several locations. I suggest that you ask the interviewee which arena she/he would prefer. Ideally you should plan to meet at the interviewee's workplace so you can have the chance to get a peek at the work environment. This allows you to get a more complete picture of the climate of the office and/or industry. If, for some reason, that's not possible, you can also meet at some other mutually convenient location. If a personal meeting is not possible, you can schedule a phone appointment or communicate via E-mail.

In addition to formal interviews, you can conduct a variation of the informational interview in group settings. For instance, you can network in a similar fashion when attending professional association meetings and alumni receptions at your particular school. Rather than having a prearranged appointment with a particular person, you can mingle at these events and make contact with a number of individuals.

Identify Low Threat Contacts

To start with, you should target people who are in career fields that interest you. Your possible contacts can be found through the strategies listed earlier in this chapter. These are the people who can give you valuable information about a job or career field. A good suggestion for those who are new at this and perhaps a little nervous about the process is to identify "low threat" people as your first networking contacts. These individuals can include family and friends, as well as contacts in unrelated fields. Through first networking with people you know or feel more comfortable with, you can practice your technique before doing the "real thing."

2

The Essentials of Effective Networking

Yes, there is research to be done before you start frolicking down the networking road! In fact, lack of appropriate research is the single biggest pitfall to networking effectively. Many people erroneously assume that because a networking opportunity is not an actual job interview, it's okay not to really be prepared for it. WRONG! You never know what can result from such a meeting, so it's always best to present yourself in the best possible light. This means knowing what you want, knowing what you have to offer, and presenting what you have to offer in a clear, concise summary of your skills, known as a resume.

Know Thyself

In order to effectively network, you must know *why* you're networking. In other words, what is it you hope to gain by meeting with these networking contacts? Are you trying to decide what career is best for you? Or are you more interested in making contacts in your field of interest for the job search? In order to make the networking process work for you, you must first determine what your goal is.

Now, don't freak out. I'm not saying that you need to know *today* exactly what you want to do with your career. In some cases, that's why you want to network to begin with. What I am saying is you need to know *why* you want to meet with your networking contacts. Networking can serve a variety of purposes, depending on where you are in your job search. Take Lisa, for example. Lisa was in her sophomore year of college and was trying to decide if she wanted to pursue a career in law or social services. From conducting research through reading up on both professions, she found them both to be attractive choices. Her goal for networking was to get some personal accounts about what those jobs actually entailed. She felt that this information would better help her decide the career path she wanted to pursue.

Karl, on the other hand, decided at age twenty-five to change careers. He had been teaching high school English for four years and decided he wasn't happy conjugating nouns and verbs all day. He had been editor-in-chief of his college newspaper, and decided that he wanted to return to his passion for journalism. His goal for networking was more focused, so he was targeting his networking efforts on people working in those jobs alone. He wanted to cultivate contacts in the field in an effort to determine where the actual jobs might be.

But just as important as figuring out what you want to get out of your networking experiences is determining what you have to offer. Networking, regardless of your motivations, requires that you be familiar with the "language of you." What does that mean, you might ask? Before starting any job search, you want to first take an honest look at yourself. This process of self-assessment allows you to evaluate your skills, accomplishments, interests, and values. Knowing yourself will better help you determine what career is the best fit for you and allow you to convey this self-knowledge to networking contacts and potential employers.

What if I'm a junior in college and I don't really have anything to put on my resume?

When first creating a resume, a lot of people feel the same way you do. But often, after some thought and discussion, they realize that all of those part-time jobs, volunteer positions, and extracurricular activities really add up. Take some time to write down all of the activities you've been involved in for the past five to ten years. You may not include all of them on your final resume, but it gives you a starting point.

There are a variety of ways to assess what you have to offer. You may elect to take standardized assessment tests through a career counselor or career center, which can focus on interests, skills, and values. Or, you can simply identify some of these characteristics in yourself by reflecting on your own experiences and completing the following informal paper and pencil exercises.

To facilitate self-assessment, you need to ask yourself some basic questions. In preparation for this, it's wise to examine academic courses or programs in which you have excelled, as well as previous jobs, extracurricular activities and hobbies that you have enjoyed. Take a minute to reflect on the questions listed below. If you get stuck, have a trusted friend or family member help you with the exercise. Sometimes others can provide some objective insights into the matter!

What have been some major accomplishments in my life?

Take a minute to reflect on your life. What are you most proud of? These accomplishments can be school-related, job-related or things you have done in your spare time.

____________________ ____________________

____________________ ____________________

____________________ ____________________

What kinds of skills or abilities do I have?

I most often hear people say, "I don't have any skills." Baloney! Everyone has skills. If you find it difficult to pinpoint yours, think back on some major accomplishments in your life that you cited in the last exercise. Think of the skills needed to accomplish those tasks. Take a look at the following list of skills, which is divided up into five different categories: Communication Skills, Artistic Skills, Technical Skills, Analytical Skills, and Influencing Skills. Try to think of academic courses, job duties, or other areas in which you have done well when identifying your skills.

Communication Skills

Written abilities/detail oriented

____ proofreading
____ creative writing
____ record keeping
____ editing
____ report writing
____ translating
____ researching
____ summarizing

Interpersonal abilities

____ advising
____ empathizing
____ coaching
____ listening
____ leading
____ counseling
____ motivating
____ teaching

Managing Skills

____ supervising
____ troubleshooting
____ managing
____ organizing
____ delegating
____ setting schedules
____ accomplishing
____ making decisions
____ control

Technical Skills

____ working w/tools
____ farming
____ carrying
____ manual dexterity
____ coordination
____ computer use
____ assembling
____ installing
____ carpentry

Creative Skills

____ acting
____ composing music
____ graphic design
____ interior design
____ painting
____ landscaping
____ sculpting
____ inventing
____ photography
____ cooking
____ creating new ideas
____ singing

Analytical Skills

____ solving problems
____ analyzing facts
____ financial analysis
____ math ability
____ investigating
____ evaluating needs
____ taking inventory
____ statistics
____ interpreting

Do your skills tend to be bunched in one skill area, or do they cross all boundaries? Do they focus on working with people, things, or ideas? The trick is to not only identify skills that you have, but to acknowledge the skills that you enjoy using. After checking off all of the skills that you possess, go back and circle those that you really like to use. Also go back through your list and put a check next to the skills you do not currently possess but would like to learn. This exercise will help you identify what you like and what you have to offer in terms of skills and abilities.

Skills can be categorized as either transferable skills or content-specific skills. Transferable skills can be *used* in a wide variety of settings and can be *learned* in all types of environments. These can include communication skills, organizational skills, or leadership skills. In fact, the skills you just checked off in the last exercise are transferable skills.

There are other skills that tend to be more content-specific and require more specialized training. These might include knowledge of the statistical computer program known as SPSS or the ability to translate between English and Spanish. Content-specific skills tend to be used in particular jobs or career fields. See if you can identify some of your own by thinking of any specialized skills you might possess. It may help to list in the left column some of the transferable skills you most enjoy using, which we just identified. Now, in the right column, brainstorm some of your specialized or content-specific skills. (Hint: think of some of your past accomplishments and/or ask a trusted person to help.)

Transferable Skills	Content-Specific Skills
______________________	______________________
______________________	______________________
______________________	______________________

What have been some strong or consistent interests for me?

What do you like to do in your spare time? If you had your druthers, what would you be doing right now? Try to think of five to eight things you enjoy doing. Once you have generated your list, take a moment to think how each could be used in a job setting (believe it or not, most can be!).

Interest	Job Setting
______________________	______________________
______________________	______________________
______________________	______________________
______________________	______________________
______________________	______________________
______________________	______________________
______________________	______________________

What's important, or what do I value in life?

Values can have a very important effect on the satisfaction you derive from your job. For instance, do you like a lot of flexibility in your day or are you more productive in a structured environment? Is money important to you, or would you prefer to be doing something that's more socially meaningful? Some things to consider are the relative value of work, prestige, money, family, and free time, to name a few. Here again, think of a couple if you can. The following list may help you come up with a list of what's important to you, but you may also think of some that are not on the list. Once you have generated your list, circle your top three values.

money or high salary	recognition
prestige	friendly work setting
intellectual stimulation	career advancement
flexible work environment	autonomy
variety in day-to-day activities	vacation
philanthropy	stability
physical challenge	competition
______________	______________
______________	______________
______________	______________
______________	______________

Reflect on your ideal career

It's also helpful to take some quiet time and daydream without barriers, such as amount of money, education, or time needed for a job. Just give yourself permission to let your thoughts roam. What would that career daydream look like?

______________ ______________

______________ ______________

______________ ______________

Is the Big Picture in Better Focus?

Take some time to reflect on your responses. Are you clearer about the skills you would like to use in a job? What interests you? This knowledge of self is necessary in order to prepare for networking opportunities and the job search. You must be able to convey your strengths and abilities to people, and that can only be done once you have clearly identified these characteristics. Remember, this is a marketing campaign and *you* are the product you're trying to sell!

Career Research

As you can see, the motivations for networking can be quite diverse. What's important across the board is conducting preliminary research before initiating these contacts. In addition to self-assessment, this research includes gathering material about different careers and organizations, for you can only make an educated decision about your future with accurate information. This information can be found through a variety of sources, which include written materials, speaking with trained professionals, and using the Internet as well as other software packages.

Written Materials

This information, which can be found through your career center, library, or local bookstores, can include specialty books on industry-specific topics, trade publications, or journals and newspapers. The following resources may prove to be useful when conducting research for networking opportunities:

Career Guide to Professional Associations: A Directory of Organizations by Occupational Field. Caroll Press: Evanston, RI. Over 2,500 organizations that cover a wide range of industries.

Dictionary of Occupational Titles. U.S. Department of Labor. This large publication offers information on specific job tasks for over 12,000 jobs.

Encyclopedia of Associations. Gales Research, Inc.: Detroit, MI. 1996. Includes over 25,000 associations and other nonprofit groups. The organizations and their members can be great resources for networking opportunities and career research. Some of the organizations may even have local chapters in your geographic region. There are usually reduced membership rates for students and recent graduates.

Jobs '97. Kathryn Petras and Ross Petras. Fireside: New York. 1996. This book offers a bunch of job descriptions in various industries, including average salaries and hiring qualifications. It describes current job and industry trends, and identifies careers that have the best long-term potential.

National Trade and Professional Associations of the United States. Columbia Books, Inc.: Washington, D.C. Annual. Includes information on over 7,000 associations, what they publish, and the names of key contacts.

The Occupational Outlook Handbook. U.S. Department of Labor. Updated every two years. This book offers an overview of over 250 occupations which account for almost 85 percent of the labor force.

Professional Careers Sourcebook. Gale Research, Inc.: Detroit, MI. 1995. Includes information on over 115 high-profile occupations. Offers job descriptions, lists of career guides, professional associations, trade journals, and industry conventions.

Regional, State, and Local Organizations. Gale Research, Inc.: Detroit, MI. 1995. Similar to the Encyclopedia of Associations, but the more than 50,000 organizations listed are at the local, state, and regional levels.

Standard and Poors Industry Surveys. Issued annually with quarterly updates. Provides general information and financial forecasts for twenty-five industrial groups.

You can also write or call professional associations and individual companies for career and organizational literature. In addition to general information, professional associations can provide contact names within the industry. Below are a sampling of some of those organizations:

General

Chamber of Commerce of the United States of America
1615 H Street, NW, Washington, D.C. 20062-2000.
(202) 659-6000

Advertising

American Advertising Federation
1101 Vermont Avenue, NW, Suite 500,
Washington, D.C. 20005. (202) 898-0089.

American Association of Advertising Agencies
666 Third Avenue, New York, NY 10017-4056.
(212) 682-2500.

Arts

American Association of Museums
1225 I Street, NW, Washington, D.C. 20005.
(202) 289-1818.

Arts and Business Council
25 West 45th Street, New York, NY 10036. (212) 819-9287.

American Federation of Arts
41 East 65th Street, New York, NY 10021. (212) 988-7700.

Business and Finance

American Accounting Association
5717 Bessie Drive, Sarasota, FL 34223-2319.
(941) 921-7747.

American Bankers Association
1120 Connecticut Avenue, NW, Washington, D.C. 20036.
(202) 663-5000.

American Finance Association
New York University, Graduate School of Business,
100 Trinity Place, New York, NY 10006. (212) 998-0370.

Communications

International Communication Association
12750 Merit Drive LB-89, Suite 710, Dallas, TX 75251.
(214) 233-3889.

National Association of Broadcasters
1771 N Street, NW, Washington, D.C. 20036.
(202) 429-6400.

National Newspaper Association
1627 K Street, NW, Washington, D.C. 20006.
(202) 466-7200.

Computers

American Society for Information Science
8720 Georgia Avenue, Suite 501,
Silver Spring, MD 20910-3602. (301) 495-0900.

Information Technology Association of America
1616 North Fort Myer Drive, Arlington, VA 22209.
(703) 522-5055.

Society for Information Management
401 North Michigan Avenue, Chicago, IL 60611.
(312) 644-6610.

Disability Issucs

Heath Resource Center, National Clearinghouse on Postsecondary Education for Individuals with Disabilities, American Council on Education
One Dupont Circle, Suite 800,
Washington, D.C. 20036-1193. (800) 544-3284.

Human Resource Council on Accessibility
1747 Pennsylvania Avenue, NW, Suite 250,
Washington, D.C. 20006. (202) 785-5222.

Job Accommodation Network (JAN)
West Virginia University, 809 Allen Hall,
Morgantown, WV 26506. (800) 526-7234.

National Center on Disability Services (NCDS)
201 I.U. Willets Road, Albertson, NY 11507.
(516) 747-5400.

Education

American Federation of Teachers
555 New Jersey Avenue, NW, Washington, D.C. 20001.
(202) 879-4400.

National Education Association
1201 16th Street, NW, Washington, D.C. 20036-3290.
(202) 833-4000.

Environmental Services

Air and Waste Management Association
P.O. Box 2861, Pittsburgh, PA 15230. (412) 232-3444.

Environmental Careers Organization
286 Congress Street, 3rd Floor, Boston, MA 02210-1009.
(617) 426-4783.

Environmental Defense Fund
257 Park Avenue South, New York, NY 10010.
(212) 505-2100.

Government

American Federation of Government Employees
80 F Street, NW, Washington, D.C. 20001. (202) 737-8700.

American Federation of State, County, and
Municipal Employers
1625 L Street, NW, Washington, D.C. 20036.
(202) 452-4800.

Law

American Bar Association
750 North Lake Shore Drive, Chicago, IL 60611.
(312) 998-5000.

National Paralegal Association
P.O. Box 406, Solebury, PA 18963. (215) 297-8333.

Medicine

American Dental Association
211 East Chicago Avenue, Chicago, IL 60611.
(312) 440-2500.

American Health Care Association
1201 L Street, NW, Washington, D.C. 20005.
(202) 842-4444.

American Medical Association
515 N State Street, Chicago, IL 60610. (312) 464-5000.

Minorities/People of Color

American Association for Affirmative Action
8335 Allison Pointe Tr., #250, Indianapolis, IN 46250.
(317) 841-8038.

Association of Asian-American Chambers of Commerce
P.O. Box 1933, Washington, D.C. 20013.
(202) 783-3599

Bureau of Indian Affairs
18th and C Streets, NW, Washington, D.C. 20240.
(202) 343-4879.

Caribbean-American Chambers of Commerce
Brooklyn Navy Yard, Building 5, Mezzanine A,
Brooklyn, NY 11205. (718) 834-4544.

National Black Chamber of Commerce
117 Broadway, Oakland, CA 94607-3715.
(510) 444-5741

National Congress of American Indians
900 Pennsylvania Avenue, SE, Washington, D.C. 20003.
(202) 546-9404.

United States Hispanic Chamber of Commerce
1030 15th Street, NW, Washington, D.C. 20005.
(202) 842-1212.

Psychology and Social Work

American Psychological Association
1200 17th Street, NW, Washington, D.C. 20036.
(202) 955-7600.

American Sociological Association
1722 N Street, NW, Washington, D.C. 20036.
(202) 833-3410.

National Association of Social Workers
750 First Street, NE, Washington, D.C. 20002.
(202) 408-8600.

Science/Research

American Association for the Advancement of Science
1333 H Street, NW, Washington, D.C. 20005.
(202) 326-6400.

National Research Council
2101 Constitution Avenue, NW, Washington, D.C. 20418.
(202) 334-2872.

National Science Foundation
1800 G Street, NW, Washington, D.C. 20550.
(202) 357-7557.

Women's Issues

American Association of University Women
2401 Virginia Avenue, NW, Washington, D.C. 20037.
(202) 728-7603.

Business and Professional Women's Foundation
2012 Massachusetts Avenue, NW, Washington, D.C. 20036.
(202) 293-1200.

National Association of Women in Chambers of Commerce
P.O. Box 4552, Grand Junction, CO 81502-4552.
(303) 242-0075.

Conversations with Professionals

Most high school and college career centers have staff who are trained in career development. These professionals can provide career counseling services and critiques of your resume and inquiry letters, as well as direction toward appropriate resources for career exploration. These offices are usually chock-full of information and literature on different careers. In addition, many offer programs such as career panels, where you can listen to individuals discuss their own career fields. If you don't live near the college you attended, find out if your school has a reciprocity agreement with any colleges or universities near you.

Can I introduce myself to speakers who have addressed topics that interest me? FAQ

Absolutely! That's networking at its best. If you feel embarrassed about doing something like that, remember that the panelists are there to share information and are often happy to talk to you after the panel is over.

You may also elect to seek out independent career counselors for advice on jobs and careers. Trained in career development theory, these individuals can offer ways in which to assess your skills and conduct the job search. As with any other professional services you use, you should inquire about their training and experience when investigating the qualifications of such individuals.

The Internet

The Internet offers unlimited opportunities for learning about careers and individual organizations. Through mailing lists, bulletin boards, newsgroups, chat groups and individual E-mail accounts, a large amount of information is available right at your fingertips. If you do not have access to your own computer or you're unfamiliar with how to use one, many libraries and career centers are equipped with them and may offer training as well. A sampling of some valuable websites includes:

AdamsJobBankOnline http://www.adamsonline.com

This service features discussion groups focused on specific topics, job listings, and other types of career services.

CareerMosaic http://www.careermosaic.com.

Includes thousands of job listings with information about each employer. You can even E-mail the employers with questions. Great for networking opportunities.

Careers On-Line

http://www.disserv.stu.umn.edu/TC/Grants/Col/

Provides career information for networkers, job searchers, and employers who are interested in disability issues.

Espan http://www.espan.com/

This site was rated best in its class by Internet Business Network. It provides access to over 10,000 job listings, as well as employer profiles and articles related to the job search.

JobWeb http://www.jobweb.org

Homepage for the National Association of Colleges and Employers, the organization that governs college career centers around the country. It offers company profiles and job listings, as well as other career information.

Jobtrak http://www.jobtrak.com/

This organization has formed a partnership with over 400 college and university career centers (they list the participating schools online). If your school participates, you can access over 600 new jobs daily.

The Monster Board http://www.monster.com/

Provides access to over 48,000 job opportunities worldwide that can be searched by location, industry, company name, or keyword. Other resources include an employer profile and a listing of career events such as job fairs.

The Riley Guide

http://www.wpi.edu/~mfriley/jobguide.html

Margaret Riley, Coordinator of Network Resources at Worcester Polytechnic Institute's Gordon Library, has compiled a directory of many of the best career-related resources on the Internet. The site has many links that will help you find both career information and job listings.

In addition to these online services, you can also purchase software packages and CD-ROMs to be used for networking and career research. Some of these include:

ABI/Inform. This CD-ROM database indexes and abstracts articles from more than 800 business and trade journals.

Infotrac. General Business File. CD-ROM database which indexes and abstracts articles from more than 800 businesses, economic and trade journals, and newspapers from the past two years.

Newspaper Abstracts. This CD-ROM indexes articles in such U.S. newspapers as the *New York Times*, *Wall Street Journal*, *Washington Post* and *Los Angeles Times*.

Periodical Abstracts. A CD-ROM that indexes and abstracts over 2,000 popular and scholarly periodicals.

Predicasts F&S Index U.S. This CD-ROM includes citations, abstracts, and complete text of articles from over 1,000 business and trade publications

I should warn here against overreliance on any one of the tools mentioned above. Rather, they should be used together to ensure that you receive the most comprehensive and accurate information in your research. This research will allow you to get the most out of your networking experiences, and will enable you to present yourself as an informed networker.

The Resume—Putting Yourself on Paper

The information you accumulated through self-assessment will also be needed when constructing your resume. There are very few things that you need to take with you when networking, but the resume is an essential tool in the networking process. A resume can serve a number of purposes while networking. One, it can succinctly provide your networking contact with a summary of your skills. Just as importantly, you can use the resume to ask for helpful job search suggestions. In fact, you should ask your networking contacts for comments on your resume. What better way to get a free resume critique?

The resume is typically an objective, one-page summary of your educational background and experiences that gives networking contacts and potential employers an overview of your accomplishments and skills. Your resume could extend to two pages if you have been out of school and in the workforce for a period of seven to ten years. It should include the following:

- Educational background
- Experiences—both paid (full-time and part-time jobs) and unpaid (internships and volunteer activities)
- Activities— extracurricular activities and other volunteer positions
- Professional affiliations (if any)
- Publications (if any)
- Skills and interests— skills are usually identified as computer and language skills, or any other skills specific to your industry. You may elect to include interests or hobbies.

There are a variety of formats your resume can take, including reverse-chronological or skills-based. For excellent, detailed resume advice, refer to *Resume Job Notes* by Timothy Haft. In any case, letter quality paper should be used, and your resume should be laser printed.

Your resume should be written and fine-tuned before you hit the networking road. Give yourself ample time to write, edit, and check it for typos and grammatical errors. There's no quicker way to shoot yourself in the foot than to offer a sloppy resume to a networking contact. Take the case of Susan. Interested in finding a job in retail sales, Susan had asked around for contacts. She found out that her mother was having a cocktail party the following night where a big shot friend who worked for a well known retail store would be one of the guests. There was only one problem: Susan had yet to write a resume. The night before the party Susan found herself hastily putting one together. She stayed up typing until the wee hours of the morning and then ran down to Kinko's to have her "masterpiece" copied. At the party, Susan patiently waited for the opportune moment to approach her target. After a few minutes of chitchat, the woman asked Susan for her resume! The woman quietly reviewed it for a moment and then asked, "Susan, were you really a candy *stripper* at Seaview Hospital? Perhaps you meant to write candy *striper*?" Needless to say, Susan was mortified and the woman was none too impressed.

After writing and looking at this blasted piece of paper for hours on end, it's wise to get some outside advice when you think you're done. After spending a great deal of time reviewing the same document, your critical skills can become less than perfect. Have friends, parents, and/or college career center reps take a look at your finished product before presenting it to networking contacts and prospective employers. You'll be happy you did.

Remember, your networking ability is contingent upon a number of factors. Research of self and careers in general is absolutely necessary before you can begin to put yourself together on paper and network effectively, even if you're still at the initial stages.

3

Strategies for Initiating Contact with Your Network

Once you've acquired a list of names, you may initiate contact with your networking resource person through either a phone call or letter of inquiry. There are certain strategies to keep in mind to ensure that you present yourself in the best way possible and get the information you need. So, let's take it from the top.

Phone Tactics

You probably think that it's pretty silly to have a section on how to talk on the phone, but people often overlook the importance of phone strategies when seeking out contacts. Often it's the first communication you'll have with a networking contact. Remember, your phone tactics are just as important as your other networking strategies and deserve as much attention.

Getting Beyond the Gatekeepers

It's often assumed that the potential employer is the most important person with whom you speak when making phone calls about networking contacts. Few people realize the importance of establishing rapport not only with the boss, but with the people who can connect you with the boss, such as administrative assistants or receptionists. Keep in mind that your interaction with these people can mean success or disaster in actually reaching your contact. Be professional and courteous with whomever you have contact.

Let's take the case of Natalie Smith, who attempted to call a networking contact, Mr. Samson, at You Bet Insurance Company. Natalie carefully researched her target company, and sent a letter of inquiry for an informational interview to Mr. Samson. A week later she followed up with a telephone call to Mr. Samson. After leaving two messages with Mr. Samson's assistant, her calls were still not returned. Natalie became so frustrated that in her third attempt to make contact, she coldly said to Mr. Samson's assistant, "I'm concerned that he has not been receiving my messages." Mr. Samson's assistant was quite insulted by the comment and relayed the conversation to Mr. Samson. He felt that the behavior was rude and called Natalie, curtly informing her that he had no time to speak with her. Remember, the gatekeepers can directly impact your success in reaching your potential networking contacts.

Frigid Responses to Cold Calls

If you're making an unsolicited contact or "cold call," and your contact is unable to take your call, don't leave your name with the receptionist. Instead, ask when would be a convenient time to call back. You don't want to leave a lengthy message with the receptionist regarding the purpose of your call, as it may be recorded incorrectly. Also, you lose the power to call back. And, simply leaving your name for a person who is extremely busy may put you at the bottom of the priority list for returned phone messages. If you're returning a call to a potential contact with whom you've already spoken, however, it's appropriate to leave your name, telephone number, and a time when you can be reached.

Phone Mail

In this day and age, many people have their own automated phone mail message service. Again, when making phone calls to networking contacts, it's better to speak to the actual person. So what happens if you keep getting your potential contact's phone message? If you have made several attempts to phone an individual, hanging up each time you hear, "This is the number of...," it's acceptable to leave a message. Just make sure that the message is short and concise. Your message could say, for example, "Hello, Ms. Rodriquez, my name is Tally Simpson. I found your name in the alumnae directory at Kent College, and am interested in researching the shipping industry. I thought you would be an excellent resource for that purpose because of your work at the BeAllAndEndAll Shipping Company and was hoping you might have some time to speak with me. I can be reached at (212) 777-2222 for the remainder of the day as well as tomorrow morning. Thank you."

When Is the Best Time to Reach You?

If you call contacts with whom you have previously had contact and they're not available, leave a time when you'll be home. Nobody likes playing phone tag, least of all a busy professional. Initiate a block of time when you know you'll be available. Also, make sure that there is no loud music or blaring television noise when you're expecting phone calls. You want to maintain a professional air, and the *Odd Couple* reruns will interfere with that.

Answering Machines

Answering machines are an absolute must for networking and the job search. Keep in mind, too, that your outgoing message is just as important. If you're in college and most of your calls are from friends and family, it's fine to have a goofy message or an excerpt from your favorite song on your answering machine. However, when expecting calls from networking contacts, professionals don't want to hear Seal (or any other band, for that matter) singing in their ear. Now is the time to have a clear, professional message on your answering machine. No music, no poems, just your name and number will suffice.

Working Nine to Five

Although there is no ideal time to reach a potential contact, there are some times that are better than others. First thing in the morning (sometime between 8:00 a.m. and 10:30 a.m.) is a time when people are usually just getting to the office and can more often than not be found near their desk/office. Also, later in the day, between 4:00 p.m. and 6:30 p.m., is a time when things generally start to slow down (although not in all professions!), and you may have more success speaking directly to your contact. Keep in mind that the length of the workday can vary among industries. Investment banking, for example, requires long hours, so you may have success in reaching your contact at 8:00 a.m. or 7:00 p.m. If contacting a high school teacher, on the other hand, you may have more success leaving a message between 7:30 a.m. and 3:00 p.m.

Making Contact with Your Target

So you've finally made it past the person answering the phone and are about to speak with your targeted networking contact. Now what? Remember, you don't have a lot of time to get your point across (these can be very busy people), but you want to cover some important details. You should be clear about your reason for making contact. Again, this may seem rather obvious, but many people find themselves stammering and stuttering when they find their contact person on the other end of the phone.

Before making phone calls for informational interviews, you need to formulate your networking *sound bite*. In essence, your sound bite is a clear, concise description of you, your reason for calling, and what you're seeking through the phone call. I suggest having a copy of your resume handy in case you need to refer to it. You may be asked to describe a past job or schedule an interview while on the phone. Your pitch should include:

1. **Identifying yourself**
   Speak slowly and clearly so your name doesn't sound like "Fat Moose" rather than "Pat Muse." You also want to be alert and enthusiastic, without sounding like a cheerleader. Remember, confidence and poise are crucial here.
2. **Your purpose for calling**
   You want to be clear about why you have made contact. This can include statements such as, "I sent you a letter of inquiry regarding an informational interview last week and am following up to see that you received it ...," or "My aunt, Samantha Stewart, suggested I contact you...," or even, "I saw you speak at the career panel at State University and I'm very interested in pursuing a career in the fashion industry." You need to set the groundwork for what is to follow, which includes:
3. **Specifics about what you want from your networking contact**
   Your response should be concise and to the point. For example, "I am interested in entering the field of international relations and thought you would be an excellent resource for advice on that topic," would be an effective statement. Yet another pitch might sound like, "I have been carefully considering a career in management consulting, and feel that you might have some helpful recommendations for someone starting out in the field. I was hoping we could schedule an informational interview, provided your time permits." You want to convey that you're interested in information and not a job. Carefully think out what you want to say and, as corny as it sounds, do a practice run before initiating your call.

Pad and Pencil Test

Keep a pad and pencil nearby when talking with potential networking contacts. This will prevent you from fumbling for these materials if an interview or appointment needs to be scheduled. Even if you have a great memory, don't rely on the old noggin for important details such as appointment time, date, address, and phone number. It's very easy to get caught up in the moment and forget vital information.

Thank You, Thank You, Thank You!

When closing your phone call, always be professional and courteous in your manner, thanking people for their time. Remember, informational interviews are not obligatory; people are doing you a favor. That's why it's very important to acknowledge their assistance and thank them for it.

Let's take what we've learned and play it out in a number of scenarios.

Gatekeeper, Contact Not In

Caller: "Hello, this is Sue Smith. Is Mr. Greenfeld available, please?"

Gatekeeper: "No, he is in a meeting. May I take a message?"

Caller: "I'd be happy to call back. Do you know when he will be available?"

Gatekeeper: "He should be back at around 2:00 p.m."

Caller: "Thank you, I'll try back then."

Phone Mail, Third Attempt

Contact: You have reached Dr. May Scuttle. I am not available, but please leave a message and I will call you back as soon as I can."

Caller: Hello, Dr. Scuttle. My name is Terry Ludwig. Sam Little suggested I contact you because I am interested in pursuing a job in medical research. He said you might be able to offer some excellent career advice since you have been conducting breast cancer research for the past fifteen years. I can be reached at 744-8776 most afternoons between 1:00 P.M. and 4:00 P.M. Thank you in advance and I look forward to speaking with you."

Actual Conversation with Networking Contact

Contact: "Hello, this is Sandra Carhart."

Caller: "Hello, Ms. Carhart. My name is Kelley Reed. I found your name through the Texas Publishers Directory. I am in the process of investigating career options in publishing and understand that you have had extensive experience working for key publishing companies, such as Spring and Knowlan. I was hoping that you might have some time to meet with me, either by phone or in person, so I might learn of the most effective techniques for conducting a job search in the publishing field."

Contact: "Well, what kind of information are you looking for?"

Caller: "I just completed my Bachelor of Arts degree in English with honors at University of Texas and have conducted several internships in publishing. I was interested in your advice for someone undertaking a job search as an editorial assistant. I know that you're very busy, and would appreciate any information you can provide."

Contact: "In fact, I'm in a meeting at the moment, but it looks like I may have some time next Tuesday at 11:00 AM. Can you come to my office?"

Caller: "That would be great. The directory indicates that you're located at 237 43rd Street on the fourth floor. Is this still correct?"

Contact: "Actually, my office is now on the sixteenth floor."

Caller: "Thank you for this opportunity, Ms. Carhart. I look forward to meeting with you next Tuesday, April 18th, at 11:00 A.M."

Notice that the caller first identified herself and how she became aware of her contact. Also, take note that she verified the contact's address when scheduling an informational interview. Even if you found your contact in the most current phone book or directory, verify the exact location before any interview.

Letters of Inquiry

An alternative to directly phoning your networking contact is to first send a letter of inquiry for an informational interview and then follow up with a phone call. Some people prefer this more formal method, as the letter serves as an introduction of you before making phone contact. That way there are no surprises and your networking contact will be expecting your call. This method also works well for people who may feel awkward about contacting people they don't know well (or know at all, for that matter). Here again, you must decide which strategy works best for you.

Addressing Your Target

Basically, you'll either be writing to someone who has been referred to you by another individual or you'll be writing a "cold" letter of inquiry. This term refers to writing to someone with whom you have not met before. In either case it's important to have the correct name and spelling of that name when sending the letter ("Was it Stengle or Stengel???"). If you're unsure of the name, whatever the reason, call first to verify.

In addition, if you found your contact names in trade publications or from what appears to be outdated job ads or organizational materials, it's always wise to call the organization to verify the name of the contact person. In any case, ask for the correct spelling of the person's name as well as his job title. Misspelling a name or listing the wrong job title could be your ticket to the "circular file." You'd be surprised how such thoroughness and attention to detail can go a long way in networking and the job search because so many people overlook these simple things.

Don't Be Tone Deaf

The tone of the inquiry letter for the informational interview should be somewhat formal and businesslike without being stuffy, and should not exceed one page. A straightforward, concise approach is more effective than a gimmicky, unnecessarily long one. Be professional without being too rigid.

Formatting for Success

The format of the letter is very important. You should use the standard business layout and make sure you have centered your letter on the page. You'll also want to type your letter on quality paper. Do not feel, however, that it's necessary to laser print your letter if you're unable to gain access to a computer. The inquiry letter can be typed on a typewriter or printed on a letter-quality printer. It should be single spaced, and have a double space between paragraphs.

Is there ever a situation where it's OK for my letter to be handwritten?

You should always type your letter of inquiry for an informational interview. Although this isn't a job interview, there's always the possibility it could lead to one, and a typed letter is more professional. In ANY job search situation, it's always better to err on the side of formality.

If there's one rule that I'd like to shout from the rooftops, it's this: There should be no grammatical errors, misspellings, or typos in your inquiry letter!! Similarly, no white-out should be used on the final draft, nor should you cross out any letters or words. If using a computer, use the spell check function and have several people proof your letter before sending it out. Unfortunately, the spell check function will not tell you that you should have used the word "from" when telling your contact that you received her name "form the alumni directory at Technical College."

The Actual Letter

Opening Paragraph

You'll want to identify why you're writing (i.e., Bill Smith suggested I contact you as an excellent resource for information on careers in... I saw your name in the alumni directory at Sperman College and am interested in learning more about a career in financial planning... I recently saw the article about you in *Museums Today* and was impressed by your knowledge of arts administration...). Be clear about how you've come to write to your networking contact. In other words, mention your referral source, whether it be another person, a professional association, or the fact that you read an article where your networking contact was cited.

Middle Section

The middle section is usually one to two paragraphs in length. In this area you'll want to include some personal information about yourself. This is not the time to document your life; a networking contact is not interested in what you've done since you were a toddler. Rather, you may want to briefly mention the school you'll soon be graduating from or your present position of employment as well as your (tentative, in some cases) future career plans. You should be clear that you're in the process of gathering information about a particular career field—not looking for a job. In the middle section you'll also want to pose the possibility of an informational interview. Do so politely, indicating that such a meeting would be at your networking contact's convenience.

Concluding Paragraph

Here you'll want to thank your networking contacts for their time and consideration. I also recommend that you have a specific plan of action at the conclusion of your letter. For instance, you may state that you'll contact them in one week to ensure receipt of your letter and to see if you can arrange an appointment to further discuss careers in.... Or, if conducting a long-distance networking search, you should include dates when you'll be visiting the area. If you won't be making a trip to the area, you may want to suggest an informational interview via the telephone, which can be scheduled through a phone call. Also, if you're hooked up and online, you could suggest corresponding via E-mail.

I suggest having a specific plan of action because many people erroneously end their letters of inquiry with statements like, "I look forward to speaking with you soon," and assume their networking contact will then call them. I can't tell you the number of clients who have told me in a defeated tone that their networking contact never responded to their letter. It's not the responsibility of your contact to initiate communication with you! Rather, you will need to follow up your letter with a phone call.

Electronic Inquiry Letters

Whether corresponding with someone close by or far away, it's acceptable to E-mail your letter of inquiry for an informational interview. Obviously you'll need to have access to E-mail and be sure that your networking contact is online, too. Always verify E-mail addresses just as you would street addresses.

Keep in mind that the format of your letter could be affected when sending it electronically, so stay away from fancy typefaces or formatting (you should avoid this stuff anyway). Because your format could be affected, it's always wise to follow up an E-mail with hard copy of your letter of inquiry. Remember, the letter should be professional both in what you say and how you say it.

Should I include a resume when sending the inquiry letter for an informational interview? FAQ

It's recommended that you do not include a resume with your letter for the simple reason that this is not a job interview, it's a meeting to gather information. Rather, I would suggest that you bring several copies of your resume to the informational interview. This way you can provide your networking contact with a list of your qualifications and while there you can also ask for any recommendations for ways of improving your resume. You might be wondering why you should bring several copies of your resume if you're only meeting with one person. Networking contacts have been known to ask for additional copies of your resume either for their records or to pass along to someone else (networking in all its glory!). You want to be prepared for such opportunities by having three to five spare copies of your resume on hand.

Cold Letter of Inquiry for an Informational Interview to a Stranger

42 Cherrystone Lane
San Francisco, CA 11222
November 3, 1996

Ms. Erin Felder
Producer
WCAT Network News
4228 Television Lane
San Francisco, CA 11222

Dear Ms. Felder:

I recently read the article in "Television Journal" dated October 31, 1996 about your innovative efforts to revolutionize the broadcast news industry. I found your comments about Internet access for viewers to be especially insightful.

I will be graduating from California College in December with a degree in communications and am interested in pursuing a career in television. I have admired your leadership in this area and felt that you would be a great source of advice for someone entering the field.

I was hoping that you could spare some time to meet with me to share some of your knowledge of the industry. I will call you next week to ensure receipt of this letter and to see if a meeting would be possible.

Thank you for your time and consideration.

Sincerely,

Sidney Hopkins

Referral Letter of Inquiry for an Informational Interview

411 Hopscotch Road
Edison, NJ 88899
March 14, 1997

Mr. Tom Jones
Peabody's Travel Agency
242 Manhattan Lane
New York, NY 11222

Dear Mr. Jones:

Lisa Woolley suggested I contact you due to your expertise in the travel industry. She felt you would be an excellent source of information regarding career opportunities in this area.

For the past four years I have worked in the hospitality industry. While I have enjoyed it tremendously, I have decided to explore my interest in and passion for the travel business. I feel that many of the skills I have honed over the last four years, such as my attention to detail and ability to foster relations with others, would be an asset in the travel field. I would like to investigate the career as a whole and would appreciate any recommendations you might have.

I will contact you next week to see if your schedule would permit an informational interview. I thank you in advance for your time.

Sincerely,

Lesley Pringle

Cold Letter of Inquiry for an Informational Interview to a Fellow Alum

584 Murray Court
Topeka, Kansas 44777
April 1, 1997

Ms. Molly Rivera
The Department of Agriculture
1717 East Drive
Washington, D.C.

Dear Ms. Rivera:

Through my career research, I recently saw your name in the College ot Kansas alumni directory. I am interested in learning more about careers in government, especially as they pertain to environmental concerns. I felt that you would be an excellent resource for career advice.

Graduating in May with a degree in environmental science, I have had an internship for the past year with an environmental consulting firm. I am interested in using the knowledge I have acquired to work in the area of public policy, and am considering relocating to Washington. Your knowledge of and experience in the field and city would be most helpful in making my decision.

I will be in Washington during the week of June 15 and was hoping that you might have some time to share with me your thoughts and recommendations. If a meeting is not possible, perhaps we can schedule a phone appointment or correspond via E-mail.

I will contact you next week to see if a meeting would be possible while I am in Washington. Your time and consideration is very much appreciated.

Regards,

Zane Kudrow

Follow-Up Telephone Call

You'll want to conduct follow-up with every inquiry letter you send out. As I mentioned before, it's up to you, not your networking contact, to follow up with your inquiry letters. What's nice about these phone calls is that your networking contacts have become acquainted with you first through your letter.

How soon should I follow up after sending my letter of inquiry? FAQ

If you send your letter through the postal service, it's suitable to follow up after one week. If you fax your letter or send it through E-mail, it's appropriate to follow up the following business day. In addition to faxing and E-mailing, you should also send a hard copy of your letter in case the letter is difficult to read once it's received. Also, remember that the format of your letter could be affected when E-mailing.

When phoning your networking contacts, you should identify yourself and make reference to the letter you sent. For busy contacts, this serves as a way to jog their memory. After refreshing their memory, it's then acceptable to see if a meeting can be scheduled.

Follow-up Call to a Letter of Inquiry

Caller: "Good afternoon, Mr. David, my name is Margaret Sidney. I'm following up on the letter I sent you last week after finding your name in the American Counseling Association directory."

Contact: "Oh yes. You indicated you were interested in learning more about careers in social work."

Caller: "That's right. I know that you're probably very busy, but I was hoping you might have some time to speak with me."

Contact: "I'd be more than happy to speak with you but I can't offer you a job, if that's what you want."

Caller: "No sir, I am not asking for a job. I just wanted to ask your advice about ways in which to enter the field of social work."

Contact: Well, I have some time next Tuesday at 3:30. Can you come to my office then?"

Caller: Yes, that would be great. Thank you for taking the time to speak with me. Let me just verify your address .. "

Follow-Up Call Resulting in an Impromptu Interview

Contact: This is Martha Silkwood, may I help you?"

Caller: Hello, Ms. Silkwood, this is Joshua Wilder. I sent you a letter last week at the suggestion of Sidney Corn to inquire about the possibility of meeting with you to discuss job search strategies in the area of graphic design. I was calling to see if you received the letter?"

Contact: "Yes, as a matter of fact I did. I am scheduled to go out of town the day after tomorrow, so my schedule is very tight. I have a few moments to speak with you right now, however. What can I do for you?"

This scenario exemplifies how you should be ready with your questions when you call to follow up. You never know when you'll be expected to conduct the interview at a moment's notice! Although your contact may be interested in scheduling an actual appointment, you should have your questions prepared and your resume at your fingertips. The next section will discuss exactly how to prepare yourself for the interview, whether it's conducted by phone or in person.

4

Making Contact—The Informational Interview

Preparing for the Big Meet

Preparing for an informational interview goes beyond just showing up for the appointment. In order to make the best impression and to remain sane through the process, you need to pay attention not only to the actual interview, but to everything that leads up to it and follows it. Take the case of Sam. After many months of telephone calls and inquiry letters, he was faced with a great opportunity to conduct an informational interview with the administrator of a well-respected hospital where he always wanted to work. But because he scheduled five interviews for the same day and didn't allow enough travel time between appointments, he showed up late to the meeting. Furthermore, since it wasn't a job interview,

Sam figured it was okay to wear jeans, only to find everybody in more formal attire. Needless to say, the hospital administrator was not bowled over. Not only did Sam blow the informational interview, but he lost out on valuable future networking contacts because the administrator was none too eager to pass him along to any of her professional colleagues.

So, in addition to actually getting the interviews, you need to be prepared for them.This means taking time to think about interview sites, scheduling, how you interact once you're face-to-face with your networking contact, and how you follow up after the interview is over.Although it may seem overwhelming, it doesn't have to be. Just take it one step at a time.

Interview Sites

Informational interviews can be conducted in several locations. The interview can occur at the workplace, at some other agreed upon location, via telephone, or through E-mail. I suggest that you ask the interviewer which arena she would prefer.

Again, it's ideal to meet at the interviewer's workplace. That way you get a chance to check out the work environment. While this is what I consider to be the best venue for informational interviews, your contact may choose another location, such as a restaurant or coffee shop. These locations are also fine, as long as both you and the interviewer are comfortable with the arrangement.

Networking can also take place at career fairs, alumni receptions, or professional association meetings, in addition to informational interviews with a single person. These networking opportunities follow a less structured format than the informational interview, but similar material can be gathered. Rather than a one-on-one meeting, these types of events allow you to chat with a number of people about their careers. Obviously, these receptions can occur in a variety of settings. Your own networking style will determine if you're more comfortable with individual appointments, group settings, or both. If attending such events, you'll need to be prepared with additional copies of your resume, depending on the size of the group. And remember, if alcoholic beverages are being served at any networking event, it's wise to refrain—you want to have a clear head at all times.

If a personal interview is not feasible, interviews can also be conducted by telephone. If you mutually decide to conduct a phone interview, you should initiate the call (unless the interviewee asks to do so). Make sure you have appointed a mutually convenient time, and phone at that time. Nothing is more aggravating for a busy professional than to be expecting a call at 11:00 A.M., and to still be waiting for that call at 11:15 A.M. Be prepared with a copy of your resume and a list of questions when calling so you're not shuffling papers during the phone appointment. It may also be helpful to have a glass of water handy in case you get nervous and your mouth begins to feel like a cotton ball.

It's All a Matter of Timing

Scheduling informational interviews, particularly as your networking circle grows, requires organization. That's why it's extremely important to take careful notes when making appointments. You should always confirm address, phone number, and time and date of an informational interview when speaking with networking contacts and, most importantly, write this information down! Don't rely on your memory for such important details. There's nothing worse than asking yourself, "Was that meeting on November 2nd at 3:00 P.M. or November 3rd at 2:00 P.M.?" In addition, you should always ask for directions if you're unsure of how to get there.

You also want to be careful not to schedule too many appointments for any given day, one of the most common mistakes I see. Happy to have the interviews at all, young job seekers overextend themselves, madly racing from one informational interview to the next. It's better to arrange fewer interviews per day so that you can be fresh and prepared for each one. Depending on the location, between two and three interviews per day is usually manageable.

Give yourself plenty of time to get to your interviews, allowing for traffic, public transportation delays, and other unexpected complications. I would even suggest padding your travel time by twenty minutes to one half hour. Although this may seem extreme, it's infinitely better to find yourself at the appointment early rather than scrambling in the door, completely disheveled, fifteen minutes late.

What if unavoidable circumstances cause me to arrive late for the appointment? FAQ

It's always wise to seek out a telephone, call ahead, and explain the situation. When people are running late, they often feel it will waste valuable time to stop for a telephone call. But those extra minutes can make up for potential angry feelings on the part of your networking contact.

Know Your Stuff

Be familiar in the "language of you" when conducting any type of interview. This means knowing why you're at the interview, as discussed in chapter 2. For some, the networking opportunity is a means to gather information about different careers. These people are in the early stages of their career research. For others, who are more advanced in the job search, these opportunities are used to cultivate contacts in a specific field in order to look for a job. If you're cultivating contacts for the job search, you should also know what you have to offer to that specific field. This means assessing your skills and abilities as they pertain to the industry, and conveying these strengths to your networking contact in the informational interview.

Remember that anything on your resume is fair game for questions. This, too, may seem rather simplistic, but you'd be surprised how some people forget small (and sometimes not so small) tidbits of information they've listed on their resume, especially if it's a job or activity that occurred several years ago.

Being knowledgeable about the industry of your networking contacts as well as their individual companies or organizations will also make a good impression. You'd be surprised how many people actually go to job interviews knowing virtually nothing about the job or company that they're interviewing with. It's this attention to detail that will make you stand out in a crowd, whether you're networking or applying for jobs (or, in some cases, both). Take the time to do your research. It will pay off in spades in the long run.

Questions You Can Ask

Being prepared for the interview also means being equipped with intelligent questions. Remember, you're the one who asked for the interview, right? You don't want to find yourself face-to-face with your networking contact with nothing to say. I have included a list of related questions for you to consider when preparing for an informational interview. You may use these or think of some of your own.

Educational Preparation

- How did you get into the profession?
- What degree/academic training is needed for a job in the field?
- Is any other prior experience required?
- What preparation would you suggest for someone interested in entering this field?

Questions for Your Networking Contact

- What do you like most/least about your job?
- What are your major duties or responsibilities?
- What is a typical day/average week like in your job?
- How many hours per week do you or your colleagues work?
- What skills and abilities do you find are most important in your work?
- How much flexibility do you have in your job?
- What are some of the problems you encounter in trying to accomplish your goals?

Questions about the Job/Industry

- What is the size and geographic location of your organization?
- How does your position fit into your organizational structure?
- With whom do you have the most contact in your organization?
- What do you think about the way the organization operates?
- Is there currently a demand for employees in this field?
- Where are the windows of opportunity within the profession?
- If you were looking to hire someone today, what characteristics would you look for?
- How long does it take to move from one step to the next in this field?
- What are the salary ranges for the different levels in this field?

Advice for You

- Do you have any special advice for someone entering this field?
- How is my background suited for a job in this field?
- Can you offer any feedback on my resume?
- What approach do you suggest I take from here?
- Could you suggest other people in the field with whom I could speak?

You may bring a list of questions to the interview, but try to keep the tone of the interview conversational. This isn't a military investigation; you don't want it to appear that you're simply rifling off questions at the interviewee. As you may have noticed, most of the questions listed above are open-ended, encouraging more of a dialogue.

While a conversation is encouraged, however, the informational interview should be treated as a serious, businesslike meeting, even if you're speaking with someone you already know.

Questions You Can Expect To Be Asked

What happens if the interviewee turns the tables and starts interviewing you? There are some general interview questions you should always be prepared to answer or discuss, even if you're just at the beginning stages of your job search. These questions may include, but are certainly not limited to, the following:

- What can you tell me about yourself?
- What are your strengths and weaknesses?
- How did you choose your college major?
- How did you become interested in this field?
- What skills could you bring to this field/job?
- What have you learned from your other job experiences that leads you to this field?
- Why should I hire you?
- What do you know about this organization?
- Where do you think this industry is headed?

My contact started rambling on about his college football team. What do I do? FAQ

Because you're looking to acquire information during the interview (and not just football stats), you should try to steer the interview wherever possible. Now, I'm not suggesting that you be rude or dictatorial, but if you find the interview is getting away from you, you should try to reign it in. In your situation, you might have said something like, "I bet you played a great game. How did you get from the football field to a career in...?," or, "At what point in college did you start considering you career plans?" These types of questions or comments can often get the interview back on track. And, with some tough contacts, you may have to do this several times during the interview!

Being able to answer these broad questions shows that you have put some thought into the career decision-making process. Try not to memorize answers because questions can be asked in a variety of ways. Rather, have general ideas for answers to questions, focusing on some of your key skills and abilities and how they relate to the industries you're investigating.

A Simple Yes or No Is Not Enough!

When answering questions, try to stay away from simple yes or no responses. Some questions may be open-ended, so they may require more than that anyway. But even so, try to back up anything you say with examples. For instance, let's say you were asked to name a skill you possess. Rather than simply stating, "I feel I have strong communication skills," you should elaborate on why and how you have those skills. Instead, you might say, "My position as resident hall advisor while in school sharpened my communication skills because I was often required to act as mediator in roommate disputes. I also worked closely with the Dean of Student Activities and other college administrators. Because of this job I feel comfortable working with a wide variety of people." Not only did you identify your skill, you gave concrete evidence of how you acquired it.

Silence Is Golden

Keep in mind that you may not be able to predict every possible question you may be asked during an interview. So, if you get thrown a curve ball, take a minute to think about the unexpected question before answering. Silences during the interview are okay. Many people feel that if they don't respond immediately to a question they'll come across as unprepared. Believe me, it's more important to respond thoughtfully than to blurt out any old answer that comes to mind.

Dress for Success

Yes, I'm finally getting to the big question. What should you wear to the informational interview? Unfortunately (or fortunately, depending on how you look at it), there is no straight answer to this question. Many people would say that you must go to all interviews in a blue or black suit. Actually, industries vary greatly in their dress codes. That's why it's very smart to do your homework and research industry trends with regard to office attire. Obviously, some industries are more laid back then others. Just as you wouldn't want to go to a law firm in jeans and sneakers, you also don't want to show up to an informational interview at an art gallery in a staid, gray suit with black pumps and a matching briefcase.

Now that I've probably confused some of you, let me try to give you some general pointers to follow when "dressing for success."

- The danger with informational interviews is that many people feel that they don't need to "dress up" because it's not a "real" job interview. You should approach any and all networking experiences as if they were real job interviews!
- You and your outfit should be clean and presentable. No food in your teeth, dirt under your fingernails, or stains on your clothes, please. And, for that matter, no gum chewing or heavy smoking before the interview either. Nothing will turn off someone quicker than a sloppy appearance.
- Investigate industry trends. How do people generally dress in a given field? I once spoke with a woman who conducts interviews for a well-known bank and who had recently interviewed a young woman for a job in commercial banking. The young woman had come to the interview in a beautiful (and costly, I might add) pants suit. While the interviewer was reasonably impressed by the young woman, she didn't hire her because she had worn pants to the interview! The interviewer felt that the young woman had not done her homework, or she would have known that banking tends to be a more conservative industry. While I am not speaking for all banks here, you get my drift. Which brings me to my next point:

- If ever in doubt, always err on the conservative or professional side. While it's hoped that you always hit the mark in your interviewing attire, it's always better to be a little too dressed up than too casual.
- You should also try to keep your outfit as simple as possible, leaving your bangle bracelets, extra rings and fragrant cologne at home. Some people may find these things offensive, so it's better to be safe. Also, wear something that's comfortable. You want to be as relaxed as possible in the interview, and the new shoes that have created a blister on your heel won't help the situation.

What to Bring to the Interview

You should always go to your informational interview prepared. This means you should bring with you a professional style pad and pen as well as several copies of your resume. You may want to write down some important points during the interview, but guard against spending the entire interview huddled over your pad writing away furiously. Have a couple of resumes handy in case your interviewee wants one or would like to forward one to somebody else. Carry these items in a small briefcase or shoulder bag. You might also consider bringing a list of questions (similar to the ones noted earlier in the chapter), especially if you're concerned that you might forget some of them during the interview. Again, you don't want to read them off to your networking contact. Rather, they should be used as something to refer to if you find yourself drawing a blank during the interview.

Practice Makes Perfect

In order to feel comfortable about the interview, you may want to write down some responses to the questions that you should expect to be asked. You should never memorize answers to questions, but you want to at least think about possible responses. It may help to do a mock interview with a friend or family member, and even consider using a tape recorder so you can actually hear how you respond during the "interview."

As painful as that sounds, it's amazing how effective a technique it is to hear yourself on tape!

The Interview Itself

Remember, the interview begins when you walk in the door of the office (ten minutes early, right?). You may be greeted by an office administrator or receptionist and, as I mentioned in chapter 3, beware the gatekeepers! Always be polite and friendly, while maintaining a professional air. You may have to wait a few minutes so, even if you're nervous, try to avoid fidgeting. Take a deep breath and remain calm.

When greeting your networking contacts, offer a firm handshake and address them by their formal name of "Ms., Mr., or Dr. So and So," unless, of course, you know them very well. Introduce yourself even though it's probably obvious who you are. Be prepared for some idle conversation at the beginning, along the lines of "Did you find the office without any trouble?" or "How are things at State University?" You should stay away from any kind of complaining or negative comments throughout the interview, lest you look like a difficult person. So, even if it took you four hours to find the office and you got a flat tire on the way, keep your responses positive!

Should I bring samples of my work or a list of my references to the interview? FAQ

Because informational interviews are not job interviews, your networking contact may be surprised if you show up with a huge notebook of your writing samples. Remember, the purpose of the interview is for you to gather information. If it turns out that your contact would like to see your materials, you can always send them to him after this initial meeting. Better to do this than to put your contact on the defensive because he thinks you're asking for a job.

Once seated in the interviewee's office, you may want to thank him again for taking the time to meet with you and explain the mission of the meeting. You can start with any of the questions listed earlier, or you may have a few of your own that you would prefer to use. You requested the meeting, so be prepared to steer it.

Below are a few general recommendations to keep in mind for all networking opportunities. They can help ensure that the interview flows smoothly.

- Know your goal for the interview. Are you gathering information about careers or using the informational interview as part of the job search process?
- Do your homework on the industry and organization wherever possible.
- Because you requested the interview, be sure to be prepared with questions. Keep the tone of the interview conversational, yet professional.
- Keep an eye on the clock. You do not want to monopolize your networking contact's time. Be courteous and appreciative of the time you're given.

Wrapping up the Interview

As you feel the interview start to wind down, make sure to thank your networking contact for her time. One of the last questions you should be prepared to ask is whether your networking contact knows of one or two other people in the same or a related field with whom you can speak. This is extremely important, especially if you're interested in cultivating contacts in a particular industry. If you make it a point to always leave an informational interview with another name or two, you're broadening your networking circle.

You may, on the other hand, be in the initial stages of career research. If you have already spoken to some people in the field and feel that you have acquired enough information about a job or career, it may not be necessary to get additional networking contacts and you should not feel that you're required to do so. Once again, this will depend on your goal for the informational interview.

You should always ask your networking contact for a business card at the conclusion of the interview. The card will serve a number of purposes. One, it will allow you to maintain a file of your networking contacts. As your circle grows, you'll be happy that you have this card to refer to. Secondly, you'll need the information listed on the business card when sending a thank-you note to your networking contact, a crucial part of the networking process which will be discussed in more detail in the following chapter.

What if I'm Offered a Job?

At the risk of sounding like a broken record, you shouldn't expect the informational interview to result in a job offer. But, it has been known to happen. If you're presented with a job offer, I would not recommend accepting it on the spot, even if you're eager to do so. At the very least, take a day or two to think about it.

A job offer opens the door and allows you to ask questions during the interview which you wouldn't otherwise ask. You can't fully evaluate an offer unless you have some crucial information about the job. Consequently, you want to be prepared with some relevant questions.

These can include:

- What are the duties of the job?
- To whom would I report?
- What is the salary for the position?
- What is the benefits package (including medical, tuition reimbursement, retirement)?
- What is the vacation schedule?
- When do you need my decision?

Do not feel that you must accept the offer simply because it was made. Some eager job seekers are so happy to get an offer that they find themselves jumping on it without giving it careful thought. You should consider the fit between you and the organization, and how the job would affect your short- and long-term career goals. It's a big commitment, so give yourself plenty of time when making your decision.

Continued Correspondence with Your Networking Contact

Part of networking effectively is keeping in touch with your networking contacts after the informational interviews or other networking activities, such as receptions and career fairs, are over. This does not mean a phone call or letter every other day to the point where you're driving your networking contact crazy. Rather, this usually means periodic communication to let them know how your general career research or job search is going. That can mean a monthly letter, E-mail or phone call, depending on the nature of your relationship as well as your comfort level with the process. If you feel awkward about this, bring it up with your networking contact at the end of the interview. For example, you might say, "You have been so helpful today that I would like to keep you informed about my job search. Would that be all right?" Most people will be generally interested in how you progress, and will welcome a periodic report. This will keep your networking circle "alive," and may reap some benefits which I will refer to a little later.

This chapter should have helped to address your concerns about the actual informational interview. Used correctly, it can be an extremely effective networking and job search tool. But even if you've made it through the interview, your work is far from over. Read on, dear networker.

5

Follow-up and Maintenance of Your Network

All right, give yourself a pat on the back for getting through the informational interview. You may feel that you nailed it, or perhaps you think you need to polish up on some areas. In any case, many people get this far in the networking game and feel that their job is done. In fact, dropping the ball at this point separates run-of-the-mill networkers from great networkers. Think about it—you wouldn't work your tail off all semester in a class only to skip the final exam. Well, the same goes here. You've come this far, but there's still some work to be done.

Your most immediate concerns after getting home and taking off your interview suit should include two things: Maintaining a notebook or journal regarding your observations of the interview and the ever important thank-you note.

Observations After the Big Meet

The informational interview will be of little help if you don't reflect upon what you learned afterward. It's wise to write down your observations, and you may find it helpful to maintain a notebook for this purpose. It doesn't have to be anything fancy, as long as you have an organized way of keeping track of your networking opportunities. Some of the information you'll want to record can include:

- Networking contact name, title, and business address.
- Time and date of appointment.
- What did you learn about your networking contact, the career industry, and organization?
- How is this knowledge aligned with your career plans and/or job search?
- What suggestions did your networking contact have for you in your career exploration and/or job search?
- Did your networking contact give you the names of other people with whom to speak and, if so, what were their names (as your networking circle grows, this can become very confusing!).
- Did you tell your networking contact that you would let her know of your progress? When should that be? It may be wise to identify a date for follow-up and note it on your calendar. Once again, as your circle grows, it's amazing how these details can get away from you unless you're organized.

This type of information is important for both the career exploration process and the job search. And, after you have conducted a number of informational interviews or other networking experiences, it's surprising how they all start to melt together. That's why I suggest you do this type of debriefing as soon after the interview as possible, while the information is still fresh in your head.

The Thank-You Note

Remember that business card you stuffed in your wallet after your interview? Well, pull that baby out. The thank-you note is an absolute requirement after the informational interview. Furthermore, the timing of it is just as important. The thank-you note should be sent out to your networking contact within forty-eight hours of the informational interview. No ifs, ands, or buts about it!

If you forgot to get a business card from your networking contact, don't blow a fuse. One of the purposes of the card is to ensure that you have the correct spelling of your contact's name, as well as his appropriate job title and company name. If you don't have a business card, you can always call the office receptionist or human resources department to find out this information. Just make sure you have it when sitting down to write your thank-you letter.

There's always plenty of controversy over whether the thank-you note should be typed or handwritten. There's no absolute answer here (is nothing in life clear cut?). Handwritten thank-you notes are acceptable if the atmosphere of the industry seems to be on the casual side or if you know your networking contact very well, *provided your handwriting is legible*. If your handwriting resembles that of a gorilla, suffice it to say that you should type your thank-you note. Like any other part of the networking process, if in doubt, err on the professional side by typing your letter.

If handwriting your note, you should do so on a simple note card. Stay away from anything flowery or too detailed. Simplicity is the key here. Whether choosing this route or using plain bond paper, make sure that the color and weight of your stationery and envelopes match. You should also stay away from wild colors like bright purple or lime green; a simple cream, white, or gray colored paper will do nicely.

Keep It Professional

The tone and format for your thank-you note should be similar to that of your inquiry letter. The standard business format and professional tone are suggested. Now if the tone of your interview was very casual, you might have some latitude with the tone of your letter, but be careful. Again, it's better to be too formal rather than too casual. The thank-you note need not be extremely long—one page will do it—and it's usually broken up into three or four paragraphs.

When starting the letter, use your networking contact's formal title of Ms., Mr., or Dr. So and So. You're free to use the person's first name only if she asked you to do so during the interview or if it's someone you know well. Inappropriate familiarity can be a real turnoff and could work against you in the long run.

First Paragraph

You'll want to begin your letter by thanking your networking contact for meeting with you. Statements like, "It was a pleasure to meet with you...," "Thank you for taking the time from your busy schedule..." or "Your time last Thursday was very much appreciated..." are good openers. You might also briefly mention what you gained from the interview, such as "Our discussion gave me a better understanding of careers in...," or "Your advice for a job search in...was most helpful." This one sentence can act as an overall summary of your meeting.

Second Paragraph

In this section, highlight or mention specific things you discussed with your networking contact and/or what you learned during the interview. For instance, statements like, "Your observations about trends in the advertising world have reinforced my decision to pursue a job in the field," or "Your comments about my resume were most helpful and I will incorporate your suggestions in my revised copy," are ways in which you can really personalize your thank-you note. These citations also tell your networking contact that you paid attention during the interview.

Third Paragraph

Those of you who are using the informational interview as a specific tool in the job search, should use this paragraph to highlight those skills or abilities which you feel make you a competitive candidate for a job in that field. Sentences such as "I feel that my strong analytical skills, coupled with my interest in the market, make the brokerage business an excellent career fit for me," or "My three museum internships and my degree with honors in art history have provided me with the skills needed in the field of arts administration," would be suitable in this section.

You could also use this section to identify how you plan to proceed from here, especially if your networking contact gave you the names of some additional people to speak with. "I will take your suggestion and contact Laura Williams next week to see if her schedule would permit an informational interview. Thank you for this additional resource," is a good way of letting your contact know how you'll proceed.

Is there such a thing as too much follow-up with a networking contact?

There's a fine line between persistence and being a pest, I always say. There's no specific formula for this one, unfortunately. A good rule of thumb is to ask yourself, "What do I have to report to my contact?" Have there been any new developments in your career research or job search? Do you have something new to report? Usually, a phone call once a month or every six weeks is appropriate if this is the case. Also, feel out your contact. Does she/he seem to welcome your calls or busy and bothered? Trust your gut on this one.

Fourth Paragraph

In this last paragraph you should once again thank your networking contacts for their time. You may also tell your contacts that you'll keep them informed of your career plans (of course, you'll only say this if you'll indeed keep in touch!). Many people will appreciate this gesture, and will want to hear what you're up to. Then it's time to sign off.

Thanks for the referrals

In addition to sending a thank-you note to the person you just met with, you should also write and thank the person who *gave* you the referral. If another individual was kind enough to give you the name of an additional networking contact, it's courteous to let that person know the outcome of the meeting. Although it may start to feel like you're writing a thank-you letter to everyone but the President, it's important to keep the lines of communication open with all of your networking contacts. Don't worry, I'll talk about how to manage the daunting task of maintaining all of this correspondence later in the chapter.

Sample Thank-you Note

July 10, 1996
25 Eighth Street
Red Bank, NJ 07777

Mr. Rip Van Winkle
Vice President
Barclay Insurance
51 Turner Avenue
Red Bank, NJ 07777

Dear Mr. Van Winkle:

Thank you for taking the time to meet with me on Tuesday and providing me with advice about entering the life insurance business. Your comments were insightful and gave me a strategy for beginning my job search. Your critique of my resume was especially helpful, and I have already incorporated the changes you suggested. Sharing with me your own early job search also gave me pointers to use in my own. At your suggestion, I will contact Mr. Rory Bowling later this week to see if he might have time to meet with me and share his knowledge of the industry.

Thank you again, Mr. Van Winkle. You have provided me with great tools for my job search. I will keep you abreast of my progress in the next few months.

Sincerely,

Meghan Blank

Sample Thank-you Note to Referral Source

July 10, 1996
25 Eighth Street
Red Bank, NJ 07777

Ms. Erin Teen
2525 Burton Avenue
Red Bank, NJ 07777

Dear Ms. Teen:

I would like to take this opportunity to thank you for referring me to Mr. Van Winkle about my job search in the insurance industry. I met with him last Tuesday and he was extremely helpful.

Mr. Van Winkle had some interesting anecdotes about his own job experiences and even gave me some pointers for my resume. I felt that his comments were insightful and gave me a clearer strategy for my own career exploration and job search. He also provided me with another person to speak with by the name of Mr. Rory Bowling.

Again, Ms. Teen, the time and contacts you have provided me are most appreciated and will undoubtedly be very helpful in my job search. I will keep you informed of any further developments.

Sincerely,

Meghan Blank

E-mail, Fax, or Hard Copy?

If you conducted your informational interview at a high tech firm or you know that your networking contact has E-mail, you can send your thank-you note electronically (remember, though, that the format may be affected). It's also acceptable to fax your note. Whether you E-mail or fax it, it's always wise to follow-up with the hard copy of the letter (in case the copy is not clear). If you're unsure if E-mailing or faxing is appropriate, play it safe and send only the hard copy of your thank-you note.

Maintaining Records

Follow-up is an important part of networking and the job search. It's a continuous project and one that requires organization on your part. As mentioned earlier, you'll want to record your observations after all informational interviews and networking opportunities. But, in the larger scheme of things, you'll want to maintain accurate and up-to-date records of all of your networking and job search activities.

Do I really need to schedule my time for networking activities? FAQ

You better believe it! You'd be surprised how easily and quickly time slips away from you. Treat it like another class you have or even a part-time job. I know that may seem rather rigid, but it works.

Believe me, it's a project in and of itself, and one that can get *way* out of hand if you let it. Take the case of Sharon, who was interested in a career in finance. Sharon was on a roll with her job search, and had several informational interviews with friends of her parents. She had also attended a networking reception for alumnae in finance at her college career center. While enthusiastic at these events, Sharon neglected to follow through with her networking contacts. In fact, she promised to send a copy of her resume to one of the alums who had attended the reception, but forgot all about it. As it turned out, a position opened up in the alum's office for an entry-level financial analyst. She would have forwarded Sharon's resume to the human resources department if she had ever received it. Unfortunately, Sharon missed out on a possible job opportunity.

Now not all acts of omission may be as dire as Sharon's, but you don't want to take any chances. Maintaining accurate and current records can serve a number of purposes and benefit both you and your networking contacts.

1. **Record keeping will help maintain your sanity.** Career exploration and the job search can be complicated activities. Believe it or not, keeping records can actually make your job search *easier*. Rather than shuffling through a myriad of paper piles and pulling your hair out trying to figure out what you should do next, organized records will allow vital information to be at your fingertips.
2. **You'll actually save time in the long run.** Have you ever spent twenty minutes looking for those car keys you misplaced? Or wasted an hour looking for that piece of paper with your friend's phone number on it? Imagine multiplying that one wasted task as your networking circle grows. I don't know about you, but I can personally attest to the fact that my weekly planner has changed my life. I know exactly where I should be at every moment of the day. The same holds true for you in your networking activities and the job search.
3. **Following up with your networking contacts when you say you will presents you as an organized person who pays attention to detail.** This type of organization makes quite an impression. Although I can't promise that this will translate into future job offers, you'd be surprised how it will separate you from the many people who are not as conscientious.
4. **Such careful records may also offer up opportunities that may otherwise slip through your fingertips.** I once worked with a client named Joe who had record maintenance down pat. He was interested in entering the teaching profession, and kept detailed records of every contact he had in his job search. Every day Joe organized his list over his morning cup of coffee, and reviewed what he needed to do for his job search. One day he noted

> that he had promised to touch base with a school principal with whom he had an informational interview several months before to let her know how his job search was going. Joe called the woman and filled her in on his activities. The woman mentioned that she had dinner several nights before with a fellow principal who mentioned that one of his teachers was leaving at the end of the semester. She suggested that he call the principal, and even offered to initiate contact with the principal on his behalf.

So, do you get my drift? While the informational interview and other networking opportunities are important, follow-up is just as crucial. Now some of you may feel that this is all becoming a little too complicated. How can you keep this mess together without driving yourself over the edge and into the abyss?

How to Keep It Together

Make phone calls, write letters, conduct informational interviews, maintain records, keep in touch with networking contracts—are you overwhelmed yet? You're in the right section of the book. For many people, getting organized is easier said than done. The following tips will be helpful in your efforts to keep it all together.

Have a Schedule

I have seen many people undertake networking and the job search rather haphazardly. One of my clients once told me, "This week seemed to zoom by. Just as I sat down at my computer on Monday to write a letter of inquiry, the phone rang. Then I realized that my interview suit was at the cleaners, so I had to go pick it up. After which I realized that I was supposed to send my resume to a networking contact I saw three weeks ago, but I had no good resume paper to print it on. So I had to go to Kinko's for paper. By Friday I found that I'd accomplished nothing."

Does this scenario sound familiar to any of you out there? This client was certainly motivated, but what she needed was a system for her networking and other job search activities. Create a schedule for the different parts of your job search activities by designating specific days (or parts of days) for specific tasks. For instance, you might set aside Monday mornings to write and send all of your inquiry letters for the week as well as print resumes. Tuesday afternoons could be devoted to following up with networking contacts through phone calls and letters. Wednesdays could be spent generating new networking contacts through a trip to your college career center or library, while Thursdays are devoted to surfing the Internet for career and networking information. This type of agenda provides structure to the confusing process of networking and the job search. You'll be surprised how you'll actually get more done once you have a schedule in place.

How you structure your tasks will largely be determined by your present schedule. If you're in college, you may have more flexibility than if you're undertaking these activities while working full time. When defining your personalized schedule, try to be realistic about the time these activities will take. For instance, giving yourself fifteen minutes to write three inquiry letters probably won't cut it and will only leave you frustrated. Also, try to focus on these activities during your peak level of effectiveness. In other words, if you're a morning person, try to avoid sitting down to work on your networking stuff at 11:30 P.M.

Keep a Notebook or Log

Maintaining a notebook of your networking and job search activities will make your life infinitely easier. That way, all of your information is in one place, available when you need it. In an effort to make your life a little easier, I have included what I call a "How to Keep It All Together Log." You can use this format to keep track of your networking efforts, or create one of your own. Whatever works to keep you organized is the key here.

Sample Networking Log

Contact Name:

Company:

Address:

Referral Source:

Date of Meeting:

Key Points I Learned:

Suggestions from Networking Contact:

Names of Referrals Made by Contact:

Make sure you set aside time for relaxation and fun

Some people become so fixated on the networking thing that they forget that "down time" is just as important as "up time." As I always say, you're not going to be good to anyone else if you're not good to yourself. In addition to those networking appointments, make sure you schedule time for a movie, rollerblading in the park, or even some time on the couch with the Sunday paper! You need time to recharge your batteries or you'll quickly burn out.

6

Other Approaches to Networking

This chapter identifies opportunities that allow you to gain more in-depth exposure to information about particular career fields while networking. These methods include: shadowing experiences, internships, externships or cooperative education, apprenticeships, fellowships, volunteer opportunities, and temporary employment.These experiences can not only help you network and gain more knowledge about a career field, they can also equip you with additional skills, if needed, to make you a competitive candidate for the job market. These methods can be used while in college to help you gain networking contacts for career research or your first job, as well as later in your career, providing the missing link for a different job search. Which method(s) you use will largely be determined by financial needs, time constraints, and required training for a particular job.

Experiential Education—It's All in a Name

Internships, fellowships, externships or cooperative education programs, apprenticeships, community service or volunteer opportunities, and temporary employment ("temp work") can all be considered "experiential education." These terms become a complicated matter when people use them interchangeably. For instance, an internship working with a veterinarian at a zoo may also be considered a volunteer experience. Similarly, an externship at a architecture firm could also be labeled an internship. So, how do you know 1) What you should apply for? and 2) Why you should apply for it?

Many words can be used to mean basically the same thing (with slight variations). I'll try to simplify the confusion by differentiating between the terms, but realize that they all have two things in common:

1. They all have specific start and end times, and
2. They are not viewed as actual jobs per se, rather, they can be the source of information about a career or training ground/path to a job.

Let's take a look at each of these terms separately.

Shadowing

Informational interviews are usually a one-shot deal. If you're interested in gaining more in-depth information about a particular job, the Shadowing Experience is recommended. No, I'm not talking about following around your potential networking/job contact in a raincoat and sunglasses. The term "shadowing" in this case refers to spending one or several days following a person through her typical work day(s). This can include attending meetings and sitting in on appointments (when appropriate). It allows you as the shadower to gain insight into a day in the life of a particular career. Those who cannot commit to great time periods might find this the most suitable method for networking and career research.

For instance, let's say you were interested in marine biology and your cousin has a friend who works for a local environmental group. Through the shadowing experience, you might be able to get a more intensive view of what a job in marine biology actually involves. Not only can you ask questions, you might be able to visit some research sites. It also allows you to come in contact with more than one of the key players at a given organization, in this case, the world of marine biology. This is networking at its best!

In order to set up a shadowing experience, you can either call or write to your contact persons. You could also preface such an experience with an informational interview. In any case, you should explain to your contacts that you're considering entering the career field in which they work and would like to shadow them for a short period of time. This task can be accomplished in half a day, one whole day, or two to three full days. It's best to ask your shadowing contacts for the specific format and schedule that would best suit them. You should be warned that shadowing may be difficult in some professions, where there is a large amount of client contact and where client confidentiality is important.

Should I shadow a social worker if I can't sit in on her counseling sessions?

Yes, I think there's still plenty you can learn from going to her office. While you may not be able to see her in action with her clients, you can still get a flavor for "a day in the life of a social worker" by observing the office environment. Of course, it depends how her day is taken up. If she's in counseling appointments for seven of the eight hours she is there, it may not be extremely beneficial for you. If, however, she has time between appointments that she can spend with you, you could learn a great deal. Talk to her about it and see what she thinks.

While at the shadowing site you should remain unobtrusive. Ask your shadowing contacts if they prefer questions as the day progresses or if you should save them for the end of the day. Remember, you're there to observe your contact persons, so keep interruptions to a minimum.

Internships

Internships are usually viewed as opportunities to gain experience in a given field, and in this case, to assist with networking and/or the job search. Longer in duration than an informational interview or shadowing experience, they can last for several weeks, to a full one- or two-year period.

I want to do an internship over my five-week winter break. Is that possible? FAQ

Every organization has different needs and requirements. Some organizations would love an intern during winter break, but others may feel that the time period is too short. Contact your organization of interest and ask if that is permitted.

Both full- and part-time opportunities are also available. Internships can be paid or unpaid, or can include some variation of the two (such as stipends, which may include a small hourly rate, or may refer only to transportation and meals). This is where it's important for you to determine your time/financial limitations with regard to undertaking such an experience.

Internships usually require some formal application process such as a resume, cover letter, and personal interview. Some internships even have an actual application which may require an essay, transcript, and letters of recommendation. For these reasons, it's important to do your research and be aware of application procedures and deadlines. Also, give yourself time to complete the applications (some can be quite lengthy). Be aware that some deadlines can be up to one full year before the internship is to start. For instance, the deadline for the U.S. Department of State is November 1 for the following summer!

Internships allow you to become immersed in a job, giving you the most comprehensive exposure to a particular career field. This method of networking and the job search is most appropriate for those who can take an extended leave from a job, or for college students and recent graduates.

Information about specific internship programs can be found by checking with your college career center, by asking profes sors, or by reading specific books about internships (these can be found at libraries or book stores). Many internship programs focus on certain populations, such as women, students of color, high school students, college sophomores, juniors, seniors, or graduates, while others are more flexible and may consider all populations. In addition, many companies list their own internship programs through their personnel or human resources departments. If you're interested in a particular organization, call them and inquire about opportunities.

Fellowships

Fellowships are typically programs for college graduates. They can be merit-based, need-based, or some combination of the two, so the competition is stiff. There's usually a formal application process that can be quite extensive. Many require academic transcripts, resumes, and letters of recommendation, so plan ahead! Keep in mind that like internships, fellowships have formal deadlines that can be up to one full year before the fellowship actually begins. The duration of these programs can be one to two years, and they usually have stipends. An example of such a fellowship program is the Peace Corps, which requires a two-year commitment and offers a stipend upon completion. Information regarding fellowships can be found at your college career center, dean of studies office, local libraries, or bookstores.

Externships or Cooperative Education Programs

Externships or Cooperative Education (Co-Op) Programs differ from internships in that they are more structured in nature and are typically part of a degree program at an academic institution or trade school. In other words, you may receive a certain number of credit hours (and a grade!) toward your degree for participation in an externship. These programs are usually a semester or year in duration, depending on the requirements of your school. What's more, you're usually paid for these experiences. Your school probably has an office (such as a career development or cooperative education center) that will assist you in finding an externship or co-op site.

Apprenticeships

The term apprenticeship is most often found in specific craft or trade careers and refers to working under an experienced person or master tradesperson in that field or trade union. Apprenticeships are usually paid, and a certain number of hours must be accrued before you can enter the field as an actual professional. People often assume that these types of programs would not be appropriate for college students or postgraduates, but if you're interested in trades as varied as carpentry or hat making, an apprenticeship might be just up your alley! Take Paul, a young man who was finishing his degree in political science at a well-known university. He'd always enjoyed building things, making bookshelves and chests for family and friends during summer months and vacations. Even though he had done an internship at a law firm while in college, upon graduation he felt unfocused, and had no real interest in pursuing what he called the "law thing." After careful consideration, he decided to apprentice with a carpenter in town. He's now a successful (and content) carpenter with his own business.

If interested in such programs, you should contact a career center, career counselor, or inquire with associations related to the field. Information about these trade organizations can also be found at your local library.

Volunteer Positions/Community Service

Volunteering or community service at a homeless shelter or a community health organization often allows the flexibility of working beyond the regular 9:00 a.m. to 5:00 p.m. job constraints, as well as on weekends. These types of positions can also be a great way to meet contacts and conduct a job search. Sue, one of my clients, was working in financial services and was interested in making a career change. She thought she wanted to pursue a job with a focus on women's issues. It seemed interesting, a place where she could make a difference, but she had little experience in that area. Sue didn't have the economic flexibility to leave her current job, nor did she have the time during the week to conduct an internship. I suggested that she volunteer at a local women's health clinic on weekends to see if women's issues was in fact a solid career interest and to gain experience in the field. The volunteer experience solidified Sue's interest and allowed her to acquire relevant skills which made her more marketable in her job search. She ultimately left her job in financial services and now runs a battered women's shelter in Chicago.

Information about such opportunities can be found at libraries, colleges, community organizations, or hospitals. This type of career exploration is beneficial for people with full-time job commitments.

Temporary Employment or "Temp Work"

Temporary employment can be a great way to meet people in a particular industry, pick up some additional skills, and get paid for it! It can also be a way to get your foot in the door in certain career fields. There are temporary agencies that focus on short-term assignments, and some that may target both temporary and permanent positions. Sometimes these temporary agencies specialize by industry, so it's wise to do your homework when researching these opportunities.

There are some shady temp agencies out there, so pay attention when deciding which one to use. You can usually find out which ones are on the up and up by asking for referrals from companies who use such agencies (also refer to *Job Smart* for more detailed information about these agencies). You will undoubtedly be required to complete an application asking for your educational background and employment history. You may also be required to take a computer skills test to determine your word processing skills or spreadsheet knowledge, because these skills are often necessary in a variety of industries. After interviewing you, temporary agency reps will try to match you with positions they have listed. You'll then have to interview at the respective organizations for these temporary jobs.

I'm Here, Now What?

Well, now that I've defined the different types of experiential education/job search opportunities, let's talk about what to do once you get there. It's not only important to acquire these opportunities, but make use of them while you're there. What does this mean? Not only are you there to do a great job, you're there to make contacts for the job search. Here are a few tips to make that a reality:

1. **Act professionally while there**
   As with informational interviews, dress in appropriate, job-related attire. Be punctual and adhere to your schedule, and don't use company time for personal concerns. If you find yourself with free time, ask if there are other projects to get involved in. Or, initiate a project of your own! Nothing is more impressive than an intern/fellow/apprentice/volunteer who has obviously found an area that needs attention and takes it upon himself to tackle the issue. Of course, it's proper to ask for permission first before taking on any new project.
2. **Make contacts while at your internship/fellowship/apprentice/volunteer site**
   Talk to people! It's hoped that these are the networking contacts that will ultimately assist you with your career decisions. Be professional, but don't be shy. Whether it is the president of the company or other office workers, introduce yourself.
3. **Gather information about the entire industry while there**
   Don't just assume you can only learn about the company you work with—branch out and ask questions about other organizations in that particular industry. It's also smart to make contact with people at related organizations.

In an environment where the economy is tight and the job search competitive, these types of experiential education can not only provide you with amazing networking opportunities, they can make you a more skilled candidate for the job search!

CONCLUSION

Now that we've walked through the networking process, I hope that you feel more comfortable with it. Networking is an extremely valuable component of career exploration and the job search, and the information and skills you can acquire are limitless. And the wonderful thing about it is that it can serve a variety of purposes. From giving you information about a particular industry to increasing your potential job search contacts, networking greatly increases your chances of finding the right career for you *and* uncovering the jobs within that career.

In addition to the traditional networking paths, technology has opened a whole new dimension to the process. For many of you, E-mail and the Internet can provide a wealth of information right at your fingertips. You can conduct long-distance interviews and find information for networking without ever leaving your room, provided you have access. If you don't own a computer, you can usually find one at your college or local library. Talk about not having to ruin the tread on your new shoes!

Remember to try and use as many of the resources listed in the book as possible, rather than relying on only one or two avenues. By diversifying your networking activities you're more likely to discover the greatest number of networking and job opportunities. And for more detailed information about the job search as a whole, read ***Job Smart***, a comprehensive guide on how to look for and secure a job.

And lastly, try to keep the whole networking process and job search in perspective. You may hit some rocky spots on the road to a job, and being able to pick yourself up and dust yourself off while learning from these experiences is very important. Maintaining a sense of humor during the stressful times can also make the process much more pleasant.

So, I wish you success in your networking activities. Through a systematic approach, you can learn a great deal about a variety of career fields, increase your number of contacts in the working world and hone your own interviewing skills and job search techniques. And, who knows, you may even have some fun along the way!

About the Author

Meg Heenehan is a career counselor in private practice. In addition, she is currently the Assistant Director of Career Education at the School of International and Public Affairs at Columbia University. Meg has held the positions of Adjunct Faculty Member, Career Counselor, and Educational Advisor at New York University's School of Continuing Education. Meg has also worked at the Office of Career Development at Barnard College, Columbia University, where she managed relations with over 2,200 internship sponsors. She has prior experience as a high school guidance counselor.

In addition to *Job Notes: Networking*, Meg co-authored *Job Smart* (The Princeton Review, 1997) with Michelle Tullier, Timothy Haft, and Marci Taub.

Meg holds a M.Ed in Counselor Education from Pennsylvania State University and a B.A. in psychology and criminal justice from University of Delaware.